I Wish I Could Fix It, But . . .

Practical and Spiritual Guidance
For Those Who Love, Live with & Care for
People Who Struggle with
Mental Illness and Addictions

By
Jacqueline Castine

Phoenix Publishers
Bloomfield Hills, Michigan

© 2005 Jacqueline Castine
International Standard Book Number:
ISBN 0 943252-05-9
Printed in the United States
Second Edition.   Third Printing.
Library of Congress Control Number: 2004096537

Additional copies of this book may be purchased by
sending $18.00 plus $3.50 shipping charges to:

Phoenix Publishers
P.O. Box 7463
Bloomfield Hills, Michigan 48302

To contact the author about speaking engagements
e-mail: jycastine@comcast.net
www.jacquelinecastine.com

DEDICATION

To my son, John.

INSPIRATION

If I keep from meddling with people, they take care of themselves.
If I keep from commanding people, they behave themselves.
If I keep from preaching at people, they improve themselves.
If I keep from imposing on people, they become themselves.
                              The Way of Life, according to Lao-tzu

I gave the best twenty years of my life to my family and it has taken them
twenty years to recover from it.
                              Elizabeth Yorgen

You know you are an addicted rescuer when you are drowning and someone
else's life flashes in front of your eyes.
                              Blanche D. Al-Anon Speaker

If money can fix it—-it's not worth worrying about.
                              Tessie Freedman

I believe suicide is a function of the mind. The mind has a mind of its
own. The main business of the mind is to mind its own business.
                              Edwin Shneidmann, Ph.D., author of
                              <u>Where does it hurt? How can I help you?</u>

The hardest thing to do is to fix yourself. Fixing others is a distraction from
that spiritual task. The illusion that my life can't work until all my loved ones
are safe, happy, productive is another way of postponing life, the central fact
of which is your own deal with God.
                              Linda Brown

TABLE OF CONTENTS

ACKNOWLEDGEMENTS

A heart full of thanks to my three children, who brought me to the end of myself. Without their struggles, I might never have found God.

Many friends, acquaintances and strangers shared with me their pain, guilt, fear, anger and love, as they wrote or spoke about trying to fix, change, save or rescue another person. They all said it was hard—-hard to live it and hard to write about it.

My colleagues at Oakland County Community Mental Health Authority supported me, and this project, with patience and enthusiasm. Extraordinary support came from my team mates: Vicki Suder, Sherri Rushman.

More encouragement came from Linda Brown, Melanie Harbison, Henry Gallmeyer, Cynthia Wilson, Katherine Blasius, Dottie Eicker, Judy Walton, Eliza Taylor McMeans and especially, Jeannine Jezierski.

Graphic Design was in the capable hands of Angie Hernandez.

Heidi Kapsokavathis has been simultaneously a valued, compassionate friend and a tough critic throughout this process.

The following people spent many hours "dotting the 'i's' and crossing the 't's'": Robert Dillaber, Christine Horstman, Suzanne LaChance and Jennifer Muller.

The scriptural teaching of Pastors Dan Lewis and Jon Enright at Troy Christian Chapel has contributed greatly to my spiritual growth. The love and fellowship there has been a blessing to me in times of joy and in times of trouble.

The Word of God tells us that "the last will be first." Thus, in closing my gratitude list, I want to praise God for His love for us all and for the gift of His Son, my personal Savior, Jesus Christ. This relationship covers my mistakes and saves me from the responsibility of playing God.

INTRODUCTION

It has been fifteen years since <u>Recovery from Rescuing</u> was published by Health Communications, Inc., in 1989. I wrote that book in order to share what I had learned, and what I had not learned, through the experience of my son's serious behavioral problems and substance abuse. That title is out of print but I continue to get calls for it. I have heard it said that we "*teach what we need to learn.*" I am more than humbled to say that a decade and a half later, I am still learning and writing about the same topic. The French say, "*Plus ca change, plus c'est la meme chose,*" or in translation, "The more things change, the more they remain the same."

Through my own experience with mental illness and my daily contact with caregivers, social workers and families of people with disabilities, I have been strongly motivated to revisit the subject. My purpose is to give practical support and spiritual resources to people who have recognized their own human limitations.

If you have already read <u>Recovery from Rescuing</u>, you will be entering into somewhat familiar territory with this new book. Many of the topics are the same but the content is enhanced significantly by four factors:

1) the fourteen intervening years of life experience I bring to these pages

2) my spiritual evolution from a New Age perspective (which was for me a search for personal empowerment) to Christianity, which I believe acknowledges my human limitations

3) the altered focus that I have gained on the subject of "fixing people," now that I am sixteen years into recovery from alcoholism and seven years in recovery from bipolar disorder myself, and finally

4) the poignant and powerful testimonies of others who have contributed to the subjects of powerlessness, uncertainty, fear and faith.

This book is written for people who have run out of options—people who have exhausted their emotional, financial and spiritual resources trying to fix, change or rescue a loved one from mental illness, substance abuse, and the related behaviors and catastrophic consequences that result from them. We, who have contributed our experiences to this book, sincerely hope that by sharing our struggles, we might bring some small measure of relief to yours. We do not prescribe for any one else's situation. As you will discover in the chapters that follow, there are many paradoxes and contradictions in what worked and what didn't work in our trials and tribulations. There is no one way that works for all. We do, however, share one common conclusion: We accept that we cannot change another person, but, with the help of a Power we acknowledge as higher than ourselves, we can change our own attitudes and actions.

When I speak to an audience, I like to get them involved during my opening remarks. I usually do this by asking some questions and listening to their answers. It is my habit to do this no matter what the topic or how large the group. It helps break down the "podium barrier." It also reinforces that we share common bonds, are all knowledgeable on the subject and reminds us that we have come together because we are all still searching for answers. So if you are ready to be begin, let's see how these questions relate to your experience. In other words, "Are you in the right place?"

- Are you in conflict over a situation or person that you just can't change, no matter how hard you try?
- Do you wonder whether you are doing too much, or too little, to help someone get back on their feet?
- Do you feel the squeeze and pressure of too many responsibilities?
- Are you afraid that if you don't stay constantly on guard, someone you care about will lose all their money, become homeless, hurt themselves, die in an accident or commit suicide?
- Do you often wonder when, and how, to "speak your piece" and when to stay silent to "keep the peace?"
- Do you give unsolicited advice and then wish you hadn't?
- Do you think "letting go" means giving up?
- Can you detach from another's problems without ending the relationship?
- Do you wish you could convince a relative or friend to seek professional help for their drinking or mood swings?
- Do you have time and energy for a life of your own?
- Is it hard for you to ask for help? Are you much more comfortable "giving" than "receiving?"
- Do you suffer from "if only I had" or "if only I hadn't" thoughts?
- Do you wonder when to "take charge" and when to "let go"?

- Have you had a spiritual experience as a result of total and utter defeat in your life?

If you have answered "yes" to three or more of these questions, I believe you will find hope and encouragement in this book.

ORIENTATION

Please consider each chapter in this book as if it is a support group meeting, with a specific "topic of discussion."

I will act as a "facilitator" sharing some of the wisdom I have gathered from others and my own thoughts and personal experience. And on most topics, you will read the direct testimonies of others who have given me permission to use their stories. All names and identifying details have been changed.

I hope that in these pages you will find stories of courage, strength, and hope from real life people who have struggled, as you do. These words come from people who have found a way to turn exhaustion, guilt, fear, resentment, despair and hopelessness into faith, joy, peace, harmony and freedom from self condemnation. Perhaps you will hear something related to your situation, and feel less isolated and alone with your own difficulties. Wouldn't it be a blessing to gain a new perspective, new hope, and a more accepting heart for yourself and others?

As your facilitator in this reading adventure, there are some directives, I would like for you to keep in mind:

- The chapters in this book are not sequential. You can go to any topic you desire at any given time by referring to the Table of Contents and turning to the appropriate page. Sometimes I monopolize the discussion, sometimes not. Sometimes I'm the only one who shows up and you're stuck with just my commentary unless you decide to go elsewhere.
- If you have a logical, orderly mind, you may be a little perplexed at first by the randomness of the material. This is a rather accurate replication of any support group experience. The point is NOT, "Where are we going?" but "Where have we been?" and "Where are we now?" If you sit tight, you will find voices that speak to you and are relevant to your situation.
- Most, but not all, of the testimonies in this book are strongly slanted along spiritual lines. If you don't have a Higher

Power or a belief in a personal God, don't fret. You can expect to gain a good measure of experience, strength and hope from those who share. For many non-believers, the higher power is the support group itself.

- If you inspect this book closely, you may find some mistakes, perhaps in both form and content. I encourage you to bring these to the attention of Phoenix Publishers. Although we tried to make this product as perfect as possible, I am comforted to know that the Navaho Indians purposely weave a flaw into every rug they make. Knowledgeable buyers always look for the "Wabi," as it is called. They know that these skilled crafters want to assure the new owner that the product was made by human hands, not by a machine.

I am grateful to have discovered that, through support groups, that we can all change, grow, and learn from each other by accepting the common bond of our acknowledged frailties and human limitations.

FOREWORD
(Fall, 1997)

I always wondered what the term "nervous breakdown" really meant once you got beyond the euphemism. In September, 1997, my mind would not stop running, I couldn't sleep and I was contemplating suicide. I called my twin sister in Grand Rapids, Michigan as if connecting to her might be a butterfly bandage to hold together my fragile, shattered life.

She came immediately to our mother's home in a suburb just north of Detroit. The details of my "shameful" story spilled out of me uncontrollably. She already knew my retirement savings were gone. I admitted I was $43,000 in debt, because I had willingly let a minister use my credit cards for "God's work." She was relieved and said, "We've been waiting for something like this to happen. Finally, we can get you some help."

I knew my children, mother and sister had been concerned about my deteriorating condition, but they felt powerless to have a dialogue with someone who believed she had "a calling from God." I was even asking myself after ten years of sobriety, why did I have so many crying outbursts, end up in abusive relationships, get fired from jobs and make such self-defeating decisions? Why was I still cleaning houses after five years? What happened to that responsible, conscientious, talented woman that I used to be? The one who raised three children, won top awards year after year in her corporate sales career, the one who wrote two books, traveled nationally as a speaker and was a regular guest on radio and television.

In retrospect, I see that my manic phases wore the public face of a euphoric, creative, high energy, driven, full speed ahead, single-minded machine—a professional woman, recognized for skill and dedication. Why did this well-oiled machine break down? I headed for the nearest tunnel so no one could see the thick black clouds of depression.

Having hit the wall, I sat holding hands with my twin sister in the waiting room of the Common Ground Emergency Crisis Center in Pontiac, Michigan. After a ten minute wait and a 45 minute psychiatric screening, I was diagnosed with bipolar disorder. It was the label the professionals substituted, in the 1980's, for the term "manic depression," to soften the stigma.. Though the nomenclature "manic depression" calls a spade a spade and as a 'word crafter' I personally approve of that term, it was reassuring to have a diagnosis by any name and halt the slow steady downhill spiral of denial that almost killed me. I believed the doctor when she told me it was a highly treatable disorder, if I took prescription medication for the rest of my life.

The prescribed drugs worked to alleviate the initial symptoms of hyperactivity, suicidal depression, and delusional thinking. But the side effects were as mind-boggling as the illness. It took more than a year to adjust. All I wanted to do was eat and sleep. I gained twenty pounds in two months: DEPRESSING! My mind was in hibernation: SCARY! I could understand why some people don't take their medication. I filed for bankruptcy, stood in line to collect food stamps and went to live with my 85-year-old mother. SHAMEFUL! There was no more me and I hardly cared: HUMBLING!! But I felt the presence of God deeply, the love of my family daily and…I swallowed my pills faithfully.

I have been employed full time as the community education specialist on the Public Relations Team for the Oakland County Community Mental Health Authority in Michigan since 1999. I am enjoying physical, emotional and financial restoration. I am grateful for the professional care and case management I received through CMH and the public funding that makes these excellent medical programs possible for the indigent. By the grace of God, I am not in jail or dead, but back among the ranks of Michigan taxpayers! After living with other people for seven years, I am relishing the privacy and autonomy of my own apartment. It overlooks a small body of water that is a suburban semi-sanctuary for birds.

My prodigal son, who has battled substance abuse and mental disorders all of his life, is a deputy welding inspector in Los Angeles. When he's well, he's swell and when he's sick, we all suffer horribly. My daughters both live in New Hampshire. They are both married and each has three children. I wish I saw them more often. I look forward to spending summers in New England and winter in a warmer climate if I ever decide to retire.

BACKWORD
(1961-1980)

My son had been a problem child from the moment he was born. It seemed to me that he came into the world angry for having been born. What was this inexplicable pain he felt, my sweet little innocent baby boy? And how could I ease his pain when I was, at twenty-one, feeling so anxious, fearful and guilty that I had caused it? Irritability in infancy grew to aggression and hyperactivity in early childhood. With his two younger sisters to care for, a husband who was often away building his career, John's unpredictable behavior had me on the edge of what I feared the most—losing control.

I set out to find out what was wrong and got a diagnosis. "Hyperkinetic Impulse Disorder," the experts called it. I wonder to this day if I am the only mother who was happy to hear that her child had "brain damage." The label had a curious way of stilling the pangs of guilt I felt for having nurtured this condition. I preferred to believe that the randomness of nature was the villain. The experts recommended Ritalin, a structured environment and—counseling for me! I was ready to begin a long slow but steady path toward personal transformation.

John grew up. If he was difficult to deal with when he was five, things were worse when he was ten. Despite medication for him, counseling for me, many different schools, several doctors, many forms of behavior modification, there were escalating behavioral problems in school, in the neighborhood and at home. Well-meaning, but ill-advised, "constructive criticism" from family eroded my self-esteem and my ability to cope. His proneness to accidents caused me to fear for his safety; his unpredictable angry outbursts threatened me, my daughters and ultimately my marriage. Boarding school seemed the only way out. With guilt, grief and relief we sent John away from home.

Our son entered the turbulence of adolescence, and with his predisposition to drug usage, he was soon unable to function in school. We tried to find a place where he could be contained. There were several public and private schools, Synanon and eventually the military. At 17, he could not function in a structured setting and was too young to be on his own. But I had become involved in a 12-Step Program, gained some new insights and was getting ready to let go.

Two days before Christmas of 1980, I received a phone call in the middle of the night. Home on leave from the Navy, John had gone out drinking with some old friends. Awakened from a light sleep I heard his husky voice on the other end of the line. "Mom, something real bad has happened. I'm in jail. I stabbed somebody!"

That phone call brought me to my end—the last straw. There would be no more tears for me. No more searching. No more things to do. No more efforts to make. I was finished. I surrendered to my own powerlessness. I knew this difficult moment was a turning point for me. An indescribable peacefulness came over me and I was free from the struggle of trying to save him. I look back on it now as a gift. I did not know it then, but the end was truly the beginning—the beginning of my recovery from rescuing.

FLASHBACK
(January, 2004)

I could see the red light on my desk flashing all the way down the hall as I put my keys on the entry hall table. I pushed the phone message retrieval button and heard the attorney's voice. "I have outstanding news. Your son is going home today." The lawyer told me that shortly after the jurors were in the box, all subpoenaed witnesses were in court, and both sides were ready to go to trial, the Prosecuting Attorney gave in and the case was settled. "We got everything we wanted," he reported. John will be released on probation and the charge will be reduced to a misdemeanor if he goes to counseling, takes his psychiatric medication and tests clean for alcohol and drugs for a year."

In September of 2003, I learned that my 42-year-old man-child, who has bipolar disorder, ADHD, and prefers to self medicate with alcohol, marijuana, and methamphetamines, had been arrested in Los Angeles on charges of terrorist threats and assault with a deadly weapon. By the time I got the news, he had been in jail since July. The report was just the sound of the last shoe dropping. I knew he was in a manic phase of his illness when he drove to Michigan from his home in LA for my mother's 90th birthday party in June. It didn't dawn on me, until after the fact, that he didn't fly because he wouldn't have been able to travel with "his supply," had he gone by air. Even in spite of a long, sad, intimate acquaintance with his psychological and legal difficulties and my inability to make them go away, I was still surprised. Maybe "Mother" is just another name for denial.

The good news was he didn't hurt anyone; he got in an argument with a neighbor while he was high on methamphetamines and acting "crazy." He scared people who called the police. They found a knife on him.

The good news was that he had some money for a private attorney and the bad news was that we, his family, had to hire one, sight unseen, from the other side of the country. More bad news was that he had a criminal record with the potential of approaching the infamous California three strikes rule. Bail had been set at $100,000 and no one in our family was willing to mortgage their property.

The few times I spoke with him he was incoherent with rage. I knew he had started his lock up in a medical unit but was removed to a high security facility because of his unruly conduct. As his concerned, but calm, Mother, I knew what I needed to do first. I asked God's guidance for my son, and for myself, during this time. I prayed for his safety and asked family, friends, work colleagues and church communities to join in this intercession. I knew

I needed to maintain my own physical and mental stability. I wanted to strike a balance between taking charge, (using my Michigan contacts to connect to mental health advocates and professionals and corrections officials in Los Angeles County) and "letting go," (that is, reminding myself that I couldn't change the situation, his illness or his decision to deny its reality). Nevertheless, while he was in jail, I made some decisions about his financial obligations and paid his bills, with his money. The uncertainty of his situation was extremely stressful but I fervently hoped it would be the catalyst for him to get the medical help he needed.

POWERLESSNESS

...at our wit's end...

Powerless, adj.- *impotent, harmless, ineffectual, ineffective, null and void, inoperative, incompetent, inept, unfit, inefficient, inadequate, insufficient, incapable, useless, worthless, valueless, vain, futile.*
                    The Synonym Finder, Jerome I. Rodale

Helpless, adj.- *weak, faint, feeble, infirm, abandoned, forsaken, deserted, done for, alone, forlorn, desolate, adrift, guideless, friendless, fatherless, defenseless, unaided, impotent, powerless, weaponless, unarmed, vulnerable, unprotected, unsupported, over a barrel, confused, confounded, perplexed, bewildered, empty, barren .*
                    The Synonym Finder, Jerome I. Rodale

Surrender, v.t.- *to yield something to the power or possession of another; to give one's self up (as to the police); to give oneself up to some influence, course, emotion, etc.; to give up, abandon or relinquish, to yield or resign an office, privilege, or rank.*
                    Random House Dictionary of the English Language

We are most deeply asleep at the switch when we fancy we control any switches at all.

                                                    Annie Dillard

I cannot save and sanctify myself; I cannot atone for sin; I cannot redeem the world; I cannot make right what is wrong, pure what is impure, holy what is unholy. That is all the sovereign work of God.
                    Oswald Chambers, from My Utmost for His Highest

When there is nothing left but God, that is when you find out that God is all you need.

                                                    -Anonymous-

POWERLESSNESS

On the Sunday following the September 11, 2001 terrorist attacks at the World Trade Center in New York City, Dr. Charles Stanley, Pastor of The First Baptist Church in Atlanta, Georgia, delivered a telecast message to his congregation entitled, "When I Feel Helpless."

He began by saying that all of us at one time or another will find ourselves in a situation where we are totally past the point of being able to solve the problem—a place where we simply don't know which way to turn - where we are at our wit's end. We know we are out of control and fear has gripped us to the point of paralysis. We don't know what to do.

During the next hour of his television broadcast, Dr. Stanley delivered a powerful formula for moving from fear to faith. He said 1) We must cry out "Help me Father," and seek His comfort, peace and direction through His Holy Word, the Bible. 2) We need to ask God what He is trying to say to us through this situation. Dr. Stanley believes that God may be thinking:

> *"Ah ha! Just what I've been waiting for! Now I've got your undivided attention. I never thought you would run out of trying to fix it yourself. Now you have come to the end of yourself. I'm happy to hear you've exhausted all of your own possibilities."*

Dr. Stanley assures us that even though we feel powerless, by calling out to God, we have tugged on a mighty and powerful lifeline. We may still feel helpless at the moment, but we no longer need to be hopeless about the future. The Pastor encourages us to send out a request for others to fast and pray. Tell them you seek prayer, not advice. (If you do not already do so, begin now to keep a written diary of the daily blessings you receive. Then you will have this encouragement resource to turn to when you need to be reminded of His grace and mercy in your life.)

We are reminded to take our eyes off the obstacles we face and focus on the power of God. Nobody can change our circumstances like God. Stanley repeats "Be sure you have surrendered completely. No more pride, such as 'I'll manage somehow.' Or 'I can handle it.' As long as you think you can still do some little thing to maneuver the circumstances or manipulate the people involved, you are on your own.   Only when you admit absolute defeat, can God step in and prove His power."

So do not fear, for I am with you.
Do not be dismayed, for I am your God.
I will strengthen you and help you;
I will uphold you with my righteous right hand.

Isaiah 4:10

Marla O.: I could write a book myself. Our daughter, age 39, is back drinking and doing drugs again! She left her children and her home. She gave booze and drugs to her son who is now in jail, but her 16-year old daughter is living with us and made the honor roll for the first quarter. It has been a struggle though, and I worry about the two younger children who are living with their dad.

I told my daughter I was done with her and not to contact me any more. The most difficult thing I have done is reject my own daughter, but after twenty-two years, two houses, and thousands of dollars on schools, re-habs., etc. I have come to realize any further trying to "fix it" is just enabling her. The pain of losing my daughter to the drug-infested world is excruciating to say the least, particularly after the few good years we had. Am I angry? You bet I am! Angry that she betrayed her children, family, and herself.   I am hurt, humiliated and at the same time worried by her actions.   I feel incredibly helpless because I am afraid she will die. She has Hepatitis.

Peace and harmony are impossible at this time though I have finally "let go." But I have not lost my faith in God because I know that my daughter has to want to change and "fix it" herself. I have found this most difficult to write about, no sense of relief. I can only hope it might help you and your readers.

∞

How many times in my life have I been gripped by John's predicaments and the dizzying, nauseating merry-go round of "stay on and take charge or let go and jump off." When people asked me how I was doing through all of his legal difficulties last year, I would say, "fine." In February, I discovered that my hair was falling out!

When he was finally released on probation after six months, I realized the truth about my spiritual condition. All the while I had been praying for

God's will in my son's life, I really had my own agenda. I was sure God would agree that my son, who had a history of substance abuse and bipolar disorder, should be delivered into the mental health system through the terms of his probation. I quickly learned one more time what I already knew: there is usually a wide gap between what a judge orders and what the probation department can administer. John sees his probation officer once a month, pees in a jar. To my knowledge there has been no psychiatric evaluation, no psychotropic drugs, no 12-Step Programs. . . all components of my prescription to cure what "ails" him. At this point I had another spiritual wake up call and a true surrender. It was time for me to love him just the way he was. I wrote him a Valentine note that said "No matter what happens, I'm in your corner. Love you lots. Mom."

∞

Harriet C.: Nothing happened earlier that day to give me any warning, so neither my husband nor I was prepared. It felt as if I had been hit by a train coming out of nowhere. I was in the bathtub with my six-month-old when I had my first full-blown panic attack. I knew from a very young age that I was ultra-sensitive to many things and sometimes "thoughts" would cause me to get anxious in tight spaces but "panic" was not a word I would have used to describe these experiences.

When I screamed for help, my husband took the baby and I ran to the toilet to throw up. My husband and my family members referred to my condition as "a bug." But I knew that the mind racing had started before the queasiness, not after. The next two weeks seemed unbearable. I could not eat, sleep or smile. I was overwhelmed with fear, depression, and irrational thoughts. To say I felt powerless would be an understatement. Up until this point in my life, I believed that people were in control of their minds. That my very own thoughts and feelings had the power to terrify me was horrible, to say the least. But neither I nor anyone around me was ready to believe that I had a mental illness.

I accepted that my condition was outside of my control. As a devout Catholic, I knew that God was in control but it did not make the suffering any easier. Everyone around me continued to act as if nothing was wrong and I continued to unravel. Three weeks later, my Mother acknowledged that "a fix" would require much more than a few motivational speeches. I was ready to be admitted to the psych ward, but with two small daughters who needed me, I agreed to out-patient recovery at home. With prayer, a carefully measured dose of "family support," daily prescribed medications, and weekly therapy sessions, I began to feel alive again. I slowly came to realize that mental illness isn't something we choose. It is not a "bad mood," or a rough day; it is a sickness like any other—-one that affects the very core of who we are. And God willing, my family has realized this too.

∞

Linda B.: This year I have felt the terrible power of how the disease of alcoholism really has the power to suck up lifetime after lifetime. It has been a healing and a relief to get to that place of personal powerlessness where, with tears and grief, I have been able to get beyond focusing on how this illness in two of my friends impacts me and into the ferocious sadness of how the disease limits them. This surrender has involved asking God from the bottom of my heart to help them and to feel the overwhelming pain and sorrow that I cannot help them. I know with all the depth of my being that I have been willing to do anything I could. And I also know, so terribly absolutely—-that there is not one thing I can do to fix it. I am at Step One with them, the place of personal powerlessness. I can do nothing, except pray. I do think that prayers, coming from such a depth of surrender, are heard.

∞

Donna A.: Six weeks before Tyler's eighteenth birthday, I called his father who lived 3000 miles away to take custody of him. My son was so arrogant, cocky and filled with so much anger that I was exhausted from trying to hold him accountable.   Nothing seemed to work; the tighter my enforcement, the more out of control he became. Every night I prayed and asked God for help. What should I do? I was afraid of losing my baby to drugs and alcohol and even to death. Tyler moved to Florida to live with his dad and his stepmother. Maybe a fresh start was all he needed. That worked for a while, but it didn't take long before he fell deeper into the black abyss of alcohol and drugs.

We talked by phone on the weekends and he would visit during the summer. We would meet occasionally at a restaurant for dinner but he was not allowed in my home. Our relationship was superficial at best. In 1993, he called collect to ask me to intervene in a money matter between him and his brother. When I refused he uttered an obscenity and hung up. I was so angry and so hurt that I didn't care what happened to this child from that moment on. I fell to my knees and cried out "Abba, Father, What do you want me to do?   I can't do this any more. My heart is being molested by this child's spirit." I truly believe Jesus spoke to me and said "give him to me and trust me." As the tears fell from my cheeks and dampened my shirt, I knew that I had to trust God. Every day I prayed for God's will, knowing that the next time I saw my son, he might be in a morgue laying on a cold slab with a police tag on his big toe.

Three months passed, during which time I knew nothing about his life, but I continued peacefully praying and trusting God. Late one evening, his brother phoned to say that Tyler was ready to make changes. Would I talk to him? That night was the beginning of our reconciliation. I knew my son was willing to surrender when he told me "I was sitting in a crack house playing Russian roulette, clicking the trigger with a loaded gun. On the third click, I heard a voice softly say to me 'Call your mother. She loves you and she will help you'."

My son has worked very hard to clean up the wreckage from his past life. He has become a loving and thoughtful son. I am so proud of him and so thankful to God that He gave me the ability to submit my will to Him and trust that He would yield a victory for my son's life.

THE TWELVE STEPS
...from powerlessness to serenity...

God grant me the serenity to accept the people I cannot change,
The courage to change the one I can,
And the wisdom to know it's me.

-Anonymous-

THE TWELVE STEPS

Although the 12-Step Program was originally designed for alcoholics by Bill W. and Dr. Bob, the founders of Alcoholics Anonymous, it has been effectively adapted by many other groups whose members are dealing with areas of unmanageability in their lives. These include narcotics, emotions, sex, gambling, work, food, smoking, relationships, etc. The Twelve Steps have been called a "blueprint for living," and that is the reason I put this topic in this book.

I recently heard a gentleman say that he thought these principles should be taught in public schools. Although it is not likely to happen, it seems to me like a good idea for several reasons:

1) It introduces an alternative to the secular view that man's knowledge is supreme and if we can just get enough information, all of our problems will be solved.
2) Everyone will, at some time or other in their life, experience powerlessness over people, places and things.
3) It is a tool box that every person can use if they have the capacity to be honest.
4) It introduces the idea that, with the help of a Higher Power, all of us can react and respond to the challenges of our relationships and our "destructive habits" by taking a closer look at ourselves.

If you are already familiar with the Steps you have undoubtedly, heard many other people discuss how they practice them in their lives. If you are not familiar with the steps, this will be a very short introduction to the principles and their ability to heal relationships. My experience is just mine. Take what is useful and leave the rest. This chapter is meant to whet your appetite to learn more.

I've been given permission to reproduce this overview from a friend. It's his interpretation of 12-Step Recovery.

7-UPS	12-STEPS
1. WISE UP	I. We admit we are powerless over our addiction and that our lives have become unmanageable. II. We come to believe that a power greater than ourselves can restore us to sanity.
2. GIVE UP	III. We make a decision to turn our will and our lives over to the care of God as we understand Him personally.
3. 'FESS UP	IV. We take a searching and fearless moral inventory of ourselves. V. We admit to God, to another person and to ourselves the exact nature of our wrongs.
4. CLEAN UP	VI. We are entirely ready to have God remove these defects of character. VII. We humbly ask Him to remove our shortcomings.
5. MAKE UP	VIII. We make a list of all persons we had harmed and become willing to make amends to them all. IX. We make direct amends to those persons we had harmed except when to do so would injure them or others. X. We continue to take inventory and when we were wrong promptly admitted it.

6. REACH UP	XI. We seek through prayer and meditation to improve our conscious contact with God as we understood Him, praying only for knowledge of His will for us and the power to carry that out.
7. LINK UP	XII. Having a spiritual awakening as a result of these steps, we try to carry this message to others and to practice these principles in all our affairs.

Recently I was interviewed by writer Lori Olivenhain for her book, Overcoming Bipolar Disorder. She asked how my relationships had been affected by my illness and how I handled any difficulties. Without hesitation I told her that the Twelve Steps were my guide. I had become familiar with these precepts through my codependency and chemical dependency issues. I trusted that applying the Twelve Steps would clear away some of the wreckage that had occurred because of my behavior during the time that I was mentally ill. But this time I first had to surrender to the medical treatment and psychotropic drugs to stabilize my moods and remove the delusions and paranoia. Only then did I have the "capacity to be honest." I had already learned that I could not Twelve Step or pray my way of out trouble until I came to grips with my mental illness. The fact that I overcame my denial was clearly a break-through gift from God. It certainly was not of my own doing since I was "out of my mind." These are the Steps I took to restore me to sanity and to heal my relationships.

> *"Power in life is reserved for those who have become comfortable with absolute powerlessness in any and all given situations."*

Before you begin reading this chapter I want you to know that the 12-Step Program is not aligned with any sect, denomination or religion. It is, however, a spiritual program. Many who come for the first time are very angry—angry at their situation, angry at their addict or their own addiction, angry at God, and/or angry when there is any discussion of a Higher Power. They do not start out as believers. Some come, admit they are powerless, but get stuck on Steps Two and Three. If they stay anyway, out of desperation, most find that, while they cannot jump into the "Grace of God" right away, they can eagerly embrace the fellowship of other 12-Steppers as their "Higher Power." The literature says we claim spiritual progress, not spiritual perfection. It is a process. Thus many start as skeptics and as the program says, "come to believe." It doesn't usually happen overnight, but it can.

STEP ONE

We admitted we were powerless over _____ and that our lives had become unmanageable.

I have left a space in the object of the Step One statement so you can fill in the blank with whatever addiction, problem, or person that PREYS and/or PRAYS on your mind. The following paragraphs are my interpretation of the principles involved in each Step and some of the ways that I tried to practice them.

It must seem shocking to anyone who has never felt powerless to hear that power in life is reserved for those who have become comfortable with absolute powerlessness in any and all given situations. It is the admission of total defeat. This step is about surrender to our human limitations. Few of us get to this point without a long hard battle of trying to control a serious illness or addiction, whether is it to alcohol, drugs, food, tobacco, gambling or trying to fix other people's lives. Step One requires us to admit, "I can't do it. It is a humanly impossible task. In this situation or relationship I have no control." Now this is where many people step back or just bow out altogether. They think it sounds like despair and hopelessness. They want to hold on to their old ideas: "If I can't do it, if I don't do it, then it won't get done, something terrible will happen, someone will die and it will be my fault." "If I give up trying to do something, it is a lost cause." Sometimes we, who are in recovery, say, "You are free to go back to your old way of living. We will gladly refund all your misery." But those of us who stay realize that there are eleven more steps that will take us to freedom from our obsessions.

Of course it is not easy to admit powerlessness. Most of us either need, or desire to be, in control. We were raised with the values of self-determination, self-discipline and self-will. I have heard it said that the "ISM" in alcoholism and the other "ISM's,"stands for I, Self and Me. This observation hints at the fact that our culture, our pride, our fears are barriers to the surrender required of us in Step One. We suffer from an "ISM" when we are thinking about anything that consumes our mind during each waking moment and all through the night, as we toss and turn. Drop-dead exhaustion from worry and fear makes life unmanageable.

I came to my first 12-Step Meeting in 1977. I was reeling from the end of my marriage and my father's chronic emphysema. Both my husband and my Dad were alcoholic. It was a period of hyperactivity, sexual promiscuity, depression, and very low self-esteem in my life. When I walked through the doors, sat down and heard others talk about Step One, I knew I was in the right place. It was not hard for me to admit my life was unmanageable. Two years later I admitted I could not fix my son's problems. In 1988, I admitted I could not manage my use of alcohol. In 1997, I admitted I had a serious mentally illness and that I was indeed, psychotic. I am now 64 and I try to apply the Twelve Steps to the unmanageability of food and work in my life. I use these addictions as both comforts and distractions. Each new admission of powerlessness brings me back to support groups and the Twelve Step recovery process, though truthfully I am never very far away.

STEP TWO

Came to believe that a power greater than myself could restore me to sanity.

Insanity is often defined as doing the same thing over and over and expecting different results. For me, insanity meant trying to control people, places and things. As I continued to encounter life's difficulties, it became clear that I was not equipped to carry these burdens without help. Until I was in my middle thirties, I thought I could stop my husband's drinking, control my little boy's behavior and restore myself to sanity through counseling, therapy, and more information. The SELF-HELP approach is what I had to surrender in this step. I went to meetings, woke up to new possibilities and my hopes were raised because I could see that this was not just another "self-help" program. I was already too tired and depleted for that. I had literally come to the end of myself. Step Two gave me hope that there was help beyond my own resources. I couldn't go it alone any more; I needed both the group support and my Higher Power, whom I call God. Now every time I know I am in hot water, I no longer ask for more information. I yell for help!!

STEP THREE

Made a decision to turn our will and our lives over to the care of God as we understood Him.

I may be powerless over addictions, situations and other people, but that doesn't mean I can't do anything. I do have the power to make a decision.

Instead of dealing with my addictions or taking care of everybody else, I can decide to give these responsibilities to my Higher Power.

Fortunately, the God of <u>my</u> understanding is not a neutral, impartial observer but rather the powerful omniscient Creator of the Universe who loves His creatures. How had I arrived at this conclusion? It happened by "letting go." Like a woman desperately holding on for dear life to a rope because she is convinced that if she releases her grip something terrible, but unknown will happen. I discovered that when I was too tired to hold on any longer, I dropped into a much softer situation.

I have experienced the power of surrender so many times in my life that I can never doubt the grace of God. When I refused to bail my son out of jail, the Navy did it. When I had no insurance, I qualified for Medicaid. When I didn't have the energy to look for a job, one dropped in my lap. Countless miracles, large and small, have all solidified my faith that God is personally involved in all my affairs. He can provide for me and protect me and my loved ones. He has many working hands. God is present in the Steps, support groups, group members who "sponsor" newcomers and old-timers alike, the friends, the fellowship, the churches and clubs that host 12-Step Programs.

At the completion of Steps One, Two and Three, we realize that we 1) *Came* to a meeting. 2) *Came to* or "Woke up" and 3) *Came to believe*, that is to say, skepticism disappeared. As a result of this spiritual beginning we have arrived at three conclusions: 1) I can't fix it. 2) God can. 3) I think I'll let Him. The surrender of our will to a submissive relationship with our Higher Power gives us the power to turn away from our old behavior and move forward. We are ready for Steps Four through Nine, the inventory steps. I like to call them the housecleaning steps.

STEP FOUR

Made a searching and fearless moral inventory of ourselves.

Improved communication with my Higher Power and the loving acceptance of my fellows at meetings helped me overcome the feelings of guilt, failure, shame and low self-esteem that I had experienced most of my life. Without this self-acceptance I would never have been able to tackle the moral inventory with anything other than a negative self-loathing approach to myself.

So with guidance from the Higher Power, help from a "sponsor" and a commitment to rigorous honesty, we take pen in hand and begin to write. It is always a good idea to start with our positive qualities and then move over to the other side of the ledger. We know that our shortcomings have been barriers in our relationships and we want to reveal them.

"Exact nature of our wrongs," referenced in Step Five, means we want to decipher not only what we did or didn't do, but also why. To be thorough, we must uncover both the cause and the effect. Our motives are significant because they reveal the spiritual root of all our problems. When I first approached Step Four, I could easily see that I was critical and judgmental of other people. It was one of the reasons my husband wanted a divorce. But by looking at my motive for this behavior I could see that it was a defense mechanism, a means of covering my own self-loathing. Likewise, I was aware that I had not been able to meet my children's emotional needs while they were growing up. The searching and fearless inventory revealed that I did not have the resources to be a better Mother because my own needs had not been met as a child.

The "big book" called Alcoholics Anonymous suggests that we write about our resentments. These sore spots are festering hot spots that cover deeper layers of hurt, pain and anger. I have successfully used the Mirror Channel, one of the topics in this book, as a tool to uncover some of my blind spots.

It is not easy for a nervous perfectionist to accept the limitations of being fully human. But that same quirk does keep the antennae up for opportunities to grow. As I get older I find it easier to give up the burden of superwoman or sainthood, just as I gracefully gave up husband-hunting a long time ago. I just aim to be a regular person "trying to grow along spiritual lines." I believe that insight, willingness to be honest and ability to self-observe in spite of mental illness, addictions and self-serving behaviors have been God's greatest healings gifts to me.

STEP FIVE

Admitted to God, to another person and to ourselves the exact nature of our wrongs.

I write letters to myself and to God. I find a trusted friend, sponsor, sister or friend to talk to. This puts the cards on the table, so to speak. It reduces the fear and shame connected with the things that I did and the things I didn't do. I always think of it as that part of the housecleaning process that might be a little stinky. That's why it's especially important for me to be meticulous about those areas that heretofore I had tried to cover up. I truly believe that what I did wrong, or what I didn't do that was right, is not nearly as foul as what happens when I try to bury my mistakes. In my book Recovery from Rescuing, I was open about my husband's drinking problems and infidelities but conveniently omitted any confession about my own. I wanted to look good. Life is much less burdensome from self-condemnation when we share our human frailties with another person who understands. The process encourages us in our spiritual growth. I discovered that most of the people I talk to can relate to my shortcomings because they have done the same thing, or worse, or the idea has crossed their mind.

STEP SIX

Were entirely ready to have God remove these defects of character.

The first consideration when we approach Step Six is "were entirely ready." Were we? Why not? It would seem logical that we would want to get rid of the negative to make more room for the positives. But maybe I am holding on to a few—and for some very good, maybe some very subconscious, reasons. This is why I, once again, will ask God to help.

At first Step Six was puzzlement for me. I was an obsessive compulsive who had spent most of her life struggling with the constant burden of self-improvement. Of course, there is nothing wrong with self-improvement, in and of itself, but my motives were not healthy. I guess you could say the drive to be free of character defects was a life or death situation because I so desperately needed to avoid criticism, gain approval, and look good. I wanted to be "better than you" on the outside so I could stop feeling "less than you" on the inside. All of these unpleasant discoveries of the inventory were my defense mechanisms. I was both disappointed that I couldn't just call a trash hauler to get rid of my shortcomings and immensely relieved to contemplate the reality that not only did I not have the responsibility for this task, but I was inherently incapable of doing so. In secular terms, "What a break!" In spiritual terms, "Amazing Grace!"

STEP SEVEN

Humbly asked Him to remove our shortcomings.

Certainly Steps Four, Five and Six introduce us to humility. Humility is not to be confused with humiliation, although I must admit that it is not at all uncommon for a humiliating experience (such as a DUI) to lead a person into a Twelve Step program. The Merriam-Webster Dictionary describes

Humility as being, '*not proud or haughty, unpretentious, unassuming, meek, modest, lowly.*' Humiliation is defined as, ' *injure the self-respect or to mortify.* To mortify means to kill. Other lexicons define humility as '*to know one's place.*' In Step Seven, I get off my high horse of spiritual pride, release the reins of do-it-myself independence and acknowledge that I need God's help to do for me what I cannot do for myself. I "let go and let God."

It may be that the ability to practice each of these Twelve Steps gracefully is the true test of humility. As I write this today I am asking God to help me remove the habit of interrupting conversations and meetings because of the urgency of what is on my mind and on my "to do" list. Being a type A, task-oriented, self-motivated person, I frequently catch myself over-stepping the boundaries, charging in," to be exact. I do not really know if this is "self-will run riot," (which puts my needs above others) immaturity, lack of self-control, a form of manipulation, bad manners or an anxiety symptom of my chemical imbalance. Whatever the cause, I think it has its roots in fear: fear of not getting the assignment done on time. So the fear of failure, which was a life and death issue from my childhood, once again has the power to trump peace of mind and harmonious working relationships. I do believe that only God can, and will, help me overcome this problem.

Step Seven provides us with the opportunity to ask for acquittal and to receive it. One of my editors is a colleague and a social worker, raised in New York. She wrote in the margin of my manuscript, "On the east coast everyone talks at the same time. If you wait for everyone to be quiet before you say anything, you'll never get a chance to speak. I've tried to adjust my style to accommodate Midwest manners but some people probably still think I'm rude. I think I'm OK, and I think you are OK, too."

STEP EIGHT

Made a list of all persons we had harmed and became willing to make amends to them all.

Before we were restored to sanity by the fellowship and spirituality of the 12-Step Program, we may have been single-minded in unhealthy ways. Some people obsess about who hurt them and others can't stop focusing on how much damage they did to other people. This step gives us the opportunity to decipher the differences and focus responsibility appropriately.

I did three separate "amends lists" over the years. My children always suffered the most from my shortcomings, especially my inability to be fully present to meet their needs. I had too many of my own. I did not have a serious problem with alcohol when they were young, but my preoccupation with my husband's drinking was very damaging to the whole family. My latent, lurking manic depression made it very difficult for me to settle down my mind. I was unpredictable, often frightened, anxious and irritable. The most effective mind-altering substance for most of my life has been relentless activity. My children were well into adulthood when I was diagnosed with mental illness. It may have been a "no fault disorder" but I became grandiose and zealously religious. I isolated when I was depressed. All of this caused enormous barriers in my relationships with close friends and family members. My adult children legitimately felt that they had been abandoned.

I was hired and fired from at least three jobs, costing those employers several thousand dollars. I never stabbed anyone in the back but many an unsuspecting friend or business associate got a tongue lashing when I was in a stressed-out manic episode.

In addition to all of the aforementioned, I knew my own name had to be included on the list of the people I had harmed. Sometimes it belonged at the very top! Like so many caregivers or codependents, I had to recognize how negligent I had been of my own well-being. It was very hard for me to face the physical, mental and emotional abuse I heaped on myself in thought, word and deed in my attempts to please everyone and look like a saint. I was vulnerable to self-abuse and abuse from others because I needed approval so much. I hope I would not put that kind of harsh judgment, criticism and blame on anyone else.

STEP NINE

Made direct amends to those persons we had harmed except when to do so would injure them or others.

Step Nine is another giant stride in helping us to replace guilt with responsibility. And so often it is the key that will open the door to blocked relationships. Direct amends can be made in person, or with phone calls and letters. Sometimes acknowledging an offense also requires restitution to a person, a group, an institution or society. This can be done in the form of money, property, or even incarceration. The most restorative amend we can make in our damaged relationships is a change in behavior. But this is only possible when there has been a true change of heart.

In my family there are three generations recovering from addictions using Twelve Step programs. I have been the giver and receiver of formal and informal, written and oral amends to and from several family members. The practice usually benefits both the "amender" and the "amendee." But

I've noticed that there are also times when the apology is weighing more on the person making it and not of particular significance to the recipient. There have been times when an amend could not restore a relationship and I've had to accept the fact that the breach has been too grievous to heal. If I have acknowledged my part, committed the results to God, then I can move on with peace.

This past Mother's Day I received an "amends" phone call from my oldest daughter. She opened by apologizing for not having the time to get a card in the mail, but clearly she had given plenty of thought to what she wanted to say.

> *Mom, I just wanted to say I'm sorry I was so hard to deal with when I was in high school. But you were always there for me anyway. You stuck by your guns and wouldn't let me get my driver's license until you thought I had earned the privilege. You helped me get into treatment for my alcoholism and supported my recovery by letting me drop out of college and come back home when I needed that security.*

Her application of Step Nine amend was the best Mother's Day present any mom could ask for.

Since change in behavior is the best practice for Step Nine, I have tried to do a better job taking care of myself. I have come to believe that my Higher Power wants me to take care of me. And clearly He helps me do that.

The purpose of my "Wellness Plan" is to have more energy and compassion for myself and others. The Twelve Steps and the Bible are my main resources. I have also enjoyed reading about balance and order in Simple Abundance: a Daybook of Comfort and Joy by Sarah Ban Breathnach. In the past, I have experienced a lot of chaos and now I enjoy much more peace and tranquility. I have physical, emotional, spiritual, financial and mental stability most days. But I am fond of saying that, in my job, May, which is Mental Health Month, drives me crazy!

STEP TEN

Continued to take inventory and when we were wrong promptly admitted it.

If Steps Four through Nine are the spiritual spring "housecleaning," we can think of Step Ten as "daily maintenance." I can't remember who said that "housework is like stringing pearls with no knot in the end," but if we want to secure our relationships we will use Step Ten as our safety net. This precept gives us the structure to deal with conflicts and issues as soon as they come up, so fear, guilt and resentments, don't get out of control again. We don't want to lose what we have gained in our relationship with our Higher Power, ourselves or others.

This Step comes naturally to me. As an adult child of an alcoholic, I have always been hyper-vigilant about relationships. I have an active barometer which is always measuring "How is it going? How am I doing?" However, I tend to be more self critical and judgmental than forgiving and compassionate; it is still sometimes quite difficult for me to self-assess accurately. Fortunately this suggested manner of living is a process, not a one-time class registration where you buy the books, read the material, listen to the lectures, take the test and go on to graduation. As we say "God isn't finished with me yet."

STEP ELEVEN

Sought through prayer and meditation to improve our conscious contact with God as we understood Him, praying only for knowledge of his will for us and the power to carry that out.

By the time we get to Step Eleven, we have accumulated amazing evidence that our Higher Power is real and personally responsive to us. We can count many instances when He did for us what we could not do for ourselves. We have experienced many of the promises of step programs, especially freedom from the fear that brought us to Step One. These changes motivate us to improve our lines of communication with God as we understand Him. How we do this is an individual matter. Some of us read inspirational literature, some are devoted to Bible study, some of us pray on our knees, some in traffic jams. And some of us love to sing praises in the shower or while cleaning up the kitchen. All speak to God.

Many of us used to make our requests known according to our own desires, and some of us still do. I compromise by prefacing my requests with "If it is according to Your will, Father." Most of us have heard the expression "Be careful what you pray for; you just might get it." Many of us have learned from personal experience that it is best to surrender to the wisdom of the Higher Power because He has the widest scope of vision for all the possibilities and we can trust His judgment.

STEP TWELVE

Having had a spiritual awakening as a result of these steps, we tried to carry this message to others and to practice these principles in all our affairs.

 Let's break this step down into three parts: 1) had a spiritual awakening 2) carry this message and 3) practice these principles.

 At my first Twelve Step meeting I shared the chaos in my life and my feelings of depression and self-loathing. I was surrounded by open arms and understanding hearts. I guess it's what the Prodigal Son must have felt when His Father welcomed him home. So the spiritual awaking was love and acceptance, not criticism and judgment. It was also the door to a sense of purpose in my life. I began to develop the perspective that nothing happens in God's world by mistake; nothing is random and there are no "accidents." Everything has a purpose, even pain.

 I wanted to tell everyone about the treasure I had found. I was so anxious to carry the message that I'm sure I just jumped, as so many do, from Step One to Step Twelve. Practicing these principles in all our affairs means attention to the ten steps in between. I was too young in the program to know at the beginning that it takes a long time to "get it" and no one can give away what they don't have. It takes a lifetime of slow progress and long suffering patience with ourselves.

∞

Post Script to the Twelve Steps :

The preceding material is a microcosm of all that has been written on the steps and just the tip of the iceberg of my personal experience applying the principles to my life. If you want an in- depth study, read the Twelve Steps and Twelve Traditions or How Al-Anon Works. Families Anonymous, Codependents Anonymous, Adult Children of Alcoholics are other support groups which meet in most large communities and their literature can be most helpful as well.

 I hope that by not directly identifying myself as a member of any one particular anonymous organization, but rather as a person who has used the Twelve Steps as a "blueprint for living," I will not be in violation of Tradition Eleven which states: "Our public relations policy is based on attraction rather than promotion; we need always maintain personal anonymity at the level of press, radio and films."

I would not wish to undermine a way of living that has brought so much healing to so many individuals or risk causing offense to the various fellowships which seek protection from "self-promoters."

ACCEPTANCE

...what is, is...

Acceptance is acknowledging the truth, making a decision to stop fighting it and getting on with your life.

Dr. Laura Schlessinger

And acceptance is the answer to all my problems today. When I am disturbed, it is because I find some person, place, thing or situation, some fact of my life, unacceptable to me, and I can find no serenity until I accept that person, place, thing, or situation as being exactly the way it is supposed to be at this moment. Nothing, absolutely nothing happens in God's world by mistake. Until I could accept my alcoholism, I could not stay sober; unless I accept life completely on life's terms, I cannot be happy. I need to concentrate not so much on what needs to be changed in the world, as what needs to be changed in me and in my attitudes.

Alcoholics Anonymous, page 449

You can never lose something if you never had it to begin with. You were never in control and never will be. Let go of that illusion so that you can cut your losses and move on. Acceptance of the inevitable—-as difficult and painful as it might be today—-is the first step toward an authentic trade-off.

Sarah Ban Breathnach, author of Simple Abundance

Expecting the world to treat you fairly because you are a good person is like expecting a bull not to attack you because you are a vegetarian.
Dennis Wholey, author of The Courage to Change

Expectation is the root of all heartache.

William Shakespeare

ACCEPTANCE

I estimate that at least 75% of all the calls I get at my office from family and friends of people who suffer from untreated addictions and mental disorders involve the principle of acceptance. In addition to resources for the person they called about, I usually give them contact information to support groups for themselves.

I was introduced to the concept of "acceptance" in 1966 when, on the advice of my five-year-old son's psychiatrist, I went for counseling. The first session was a group. All of us discussed what brought us in for individual therapy. One woman's husband continually accused her of infidelity; another mom's teenage son was doing drugs; one of the men was angry that his wife had filed for divorce. The psychologist pointed out the common thread. All of us were there because another person was making our life difficult. In this first session we were disappointed to learn that we had little control over the ones who brought us there, but heartened to discover there was much we could do to change our response to their behavior. He recommended that we read Albert Ellis' Guide to Rational Living. I read it and I continued counseling with this same therapist for eight years.

The following is an excerpt from a newspaper column written by Bryan Golden, the author of Dare to Live without Limits:

To accept is to acknowledge, understand or regard as true. To expect is to assume, await, conclude or consider certain. Expectation can lead to disappointment and frustration. Expectations are associated with thoughts of how circumstances or people should be. You only have control over yourself. You don't have any control over other people or circumstances.

Unfulfilled expectations may elicit feelings of powerlessness. By expecting, you spend time, energy and emotions attempting to manage external circumstances. Doing so isn't possible with any dependability. You can expect from yourself. Everything else you must accept.

A common source of frustration is having expectations of others. If people fail to meet your expectations you can become stressed.

For freedom and peace of mind, expect more from yourself; accept change and the world around you. Accept responsibility for yourself and strive to improve and have a positive influence wherever you can.

$$\infty$$

Sandra M.: I live with schizoaffective disorder. Eight years ago, I became mentally ill while trying to hold down a full time job, go to university full time and raise three children alone. I pushed myself too much and ended up with no job, no school, no money and on welfare to feed my family. For five years, I drank excessively and I was suicidal many times. I didn't want to be on any pills, and I didn't want any illness. I tried, with my doctor's guidance, to come off all meds. Big mistake. I took seriously ill and was hospitalized for seven weeks. When I did get out I made many changes in my life. No more drinking alcohol, no more smoking. I try to eat healthfully and take my medications as prescribed. Mental illness affects all social circles. No one is immune. Only when I truly accepted my illness was I able to start getting well.

> *"Only when I truly accepted my illness was I able to start getting well."*

$$\infty$$

Nancy B.: I once felt like the "Typhoid Mary" of mental illness. I didn't contract the illness; I only transmitted it to others. That was back in the days when I would happily "sub" if God wanted to take a vacation. At that time it seemed that everyone in my family was succumbing to this terrible, invisible thing that removed their zest for life and robbed each of them of their personality. I was sure that I had somehow caused it. Therefore, I had to fix it. There was no question in my mind—if I tried hard enough I could make it all better.

> *"There was no question in my mind—if I tried hard enough I could make it all better."*

My life had been practically perfect. I was married to my high school sweetheart and we had four beautiful children, the two oldest adopted during an overseas transfer to the Middle East. The two younger children shared our gene pool. My husband was a rising young star in a company and job that he loved, we enjoyed a beautiful house and our lives were family centered. We went to church every Sunday. We wanted for nothing. I had it all under control.

Kim was the first to succumb to what I later referred to as "the family curse." Just before her 14th birthday, a school guidance counselor called to tell me Kim had written a suicide note. I had noticed that Kim was acting peculiarly paranoid. Her moods were mercurial and swift. The voices she heard in her head advised her to self-destruct. We began a round of treatments including several hospitalizations, most of which only served to reinforce her paranoid belief that we were putting her out of the family. She attempted suicide twice.

Her brother watched all of this in wide-eyed horror and he too became convinced that all adoptees from Iran would ultimately go crazy. He got involved with street drugs. He stole from us and ultimately became so out of control that we feared for our safety. We finally ended up pressing charges and he spent nine months in a juvenile detention facility.

At first I approached this problem in my usual methodical way. If I learned more about mental illness and conduct disorder, I could make them better. After all, it was somehow my fault that Kim and Robert contracted these psychiatric disorders. I was the only one who could save them.

But I soon found that none of my clinical knowledge significantly affected their behaviors one way or another. And then, faced with the stress of two self destructing teens, my husband also suffered a major depressive episode. At one point I had all three in separate psychiatric facilities. I participated in so much family therapy during that time I became fully "therapized." "Be a better wife to him," the therapist would intone. "But I am loving, don't cheat, keep a good home and have supported him through many moves due to transfers," I'd reply defensively. "Do special things with your children— take them places, get involved in activities with them," stated another therapist. "I already do," I'd protest. "Well," they collectively replied, "we can't help you if you aren't open to suggestions."

It soon became clear that no one took responsibility for their actions but me. All three behaved abominably and blamed me. And I was a willing scapegoat. I gladly accepted all blame and threw myself into fixing the mental health system. Sadly, despite my best efforts in that arena, budget cuts ensured that that didn't succeed either. I was the frenzied juggler keeping too many balls in the air and one by one they all hit the floor.

Two weeks before Christmas 1990, I came across a small card on the living room bookshelf that featured a picture of St. Therese, the Little Flower. It said "put your trust in the Lord." I believe it was a miracle: a message from heaven. That was the day God returned from vacation and let me know that I was officially relieved of duty. Those beautiful words made me realize I could only control myself and my own behavior. This brought me such a sense of peace and relief. Little by little I began to let go of all the worries and responsibilities that rightfully belonged to my husband, son and daughter. I knew I would never stop loving them or being there for them. I would just stop trying to change that which was not mine to change.

∞

Charlie G.: When I married for the first time, I still hadn't matured a lot and was ill-equipped to be either a husband or a father. I was strict with my step-daughter, Ginger, who wasn't very well adjusted before I joined the scene. My wife was probably too permissive, and that wasn't a very good mix. It was a time when California high schools issued diplomas for showing up. Ginger got involved in marijuana, became sexually promiscuous and survived several suicide attempts in later years. Even though my wife told me she thought Ginger was the proverbial "bad seed," I certainly contributed to her difficulties and I feel guilt for my misguided parenting.

As an adult Ginger, now almost fifty, has had numerous low-life lovers, one divorce, and two screwed up children. She has used up all of California's drug rehabilitation programs. Ginger was a hard person to love, even at age five, but I will always know I failed her as a father, despite my good intentions.

My wife left me after twenty years because of my tendencies to be angry too often and because she felt a lack of closeness. I didn't share her belief in God, but did attend church with her regularly with a good attitude. I did have a sincere attempt to find Him. We stayed married and mostly friendly for eleven more years. She died at 53 of leukemia. And just six months later, my high-IQ high school dropout son died suddenly when a wall of sand collapsed and buried him while he was digging for fossils on a California beach. More sadness and guilt feelings for me as a failed father. Remarkably, my other son and daughter are well adjusted, happily married, God-loving adults, with whom I have close relationships.

When I was 48, and separated from my wife, I stumbled onto a two weekend self-awareness training called "EST." "EST" has been the butt of many jokes, but the training in a "What is, is" philosophy did transform my life, though not immediately. One of the "EST" exercises involved splitting the 300 students into 150 pairs of two strangers. One person took two minutes to explain what his/her biggest problem in life was. The other person then had one minute to tell the other what they needed to do to solve that problem. Then we switched positions and did the same exercise again. The fascinating part is that the solutions given to 85% of the entire class were what they already knew they needed to do, but for various reasons were resisting doing.

"EST" helped me to finally come to grips with the obvious fact that I can't undo most of the mistakes I've made as a human being. And it has helped me accept the mistakes of my deceased father and my own short-sighted parenting. My only regret now (which I'm not obsessing about) is that it took me so long in life to really wake up and smell the roses.

DETACHMENT
...with anger, apathy or love...

We trade a life that we have tried to control, and we receive in return something better - a life that is manageable.
Melanie Beattie, author of The Language of Letting Go

You put your right hand in,
You take your right hand out,
You put your right hand in,
And you turn it all about.

You do the Hokey, Pokey
And you turn yourself around.
That's what it's all about!

(The games we still play!)

DETACHMENT

The well known psychologist columnist, Dr. Joyce Brothers received a letter from a mom who claimed to be the "world's best worrier." She said it helped her accomplish tasks, pay attention to details and motivated her to action when she feels overwhelmed. She thinks she is a better mom than most because while the rest of the family is sleeping, she is waiting up for her son to come home from a party to be sure he comes home safe and sound.

Dr. Joyce replied, "Sorry, but I think your logic is somewhat flawed. Some worry and anxiety is perfectly natural but . . . it is not your worrying that is keeping him safe." She recommended going to bed an hour before the young man's curfew, waking up briefly to hear him when he comes in and saying goodnight. "Sometimes, parents need to have a bit of faith in a higher being in order to have some feeling of control."

I have heard a lot of people describe the process of detachment as one step forward and two steps back. For me it was a sort of like "the hokey pokey." First, I detached with anger. I'd get involved, put my whole heart into it—then when things didn't work out, I'd pull away in disgust.

More often than not, later I would have a change of heart, think back that I may have been too intemperate and try to get into communication again. If I try and fail at the relationship a second time, I might avoid the blow-up of the former encounter, but I would detach again with a variation of the theme. I call it "detach with apathy." The relationship remains strained of course.

Detachment with love came only after I had experienced the other two forms: anger and apathy. In 1981, my twenty-year-old son called me from Texas, after a long period of being "incommunicado." He described a rather desperate situation, but I had given up giving him advice and trying to get him fixed. I listened first, and then I could hardly believe it when I said, "I know things aren't going very well for you right now, but I also know that you have the power to change that." Two weeks later he called me from a treatment center in California.

∞

Faith R.:   "You can't heal your family members, only yourself," my counselor told me.   Now, that didn't make sense. Didn't my family come first? No, my support group friends cautioned me. I could tell my husband and my daughter how I felt about their behavior. I could protect myself, but I could not fix them, nurture them or make them better. I needed to detach.

> *"You can't heal your family members, only yourself," my counselor told me.   Now, that didn't make sense. Didn't my family come first?"*

Such a hard concept—detachment! When I thought I had detached, my sponsor told me, "you're not detaching with love, you're detaching with hate." Again I learned over time, to forgive myself, nurture myself and heal myself first.

Time has gone by and I claim my healing. My husband did not die. In fact, he stopped drinking and, eventually, smoking. His blood pressure is now normal and he is enjoying life.

∞

In The Dance of Anger, author Harriet Goldhor Lerner, Ph.D. describes the struggles of Maggie, one of her clients, who was attempting to deal with her anger toward her emotionally dependent, insecure, controlling mother. Through months of therapy Maggie learned that while she could not change the behavior of another person, she did need to establish her independence, become less protective of her mother's feelings and develop a more assertive style of communication. She had to work through the fears that these changes might result in her mother emotionally abandoning her altogether or committing suicide. Lerner explains that "countermoves" are to be expected and that "hit and run" confrontations do not lead to lasting changes. Independence means that we clearly define ourselves on emotionally important issues but doesn't mean emotional distance. Thus Maggie needed to show, through her behavior, that although she will stand behind her own wants and convictions, she is still her mother's daughter and loves her mother very much. Declaring separateness and independence is not the same as a lack of caring or closeness.

∞

Dealing with my friend's Alzheimer's disease has been a major emotional and social challenge. The illness makes it difficult for him to be dependable. Before I really accepted the illness, there was anxiety connected to any movie or dinner date and I was always trying to control the outcomes so we wouldn't be late. I would call ahead. I would remind him the night before, the morning of, and/or an hour ahead. No matter how I tried to stay ahead of the game, somehow there was always a glitch. He always felt so bad and was so apologetic. And I always thought, "Next time I will ..." or "If only I had...". I could see I was driving myself nuts.

When it first started, I would get mad, period. Just as often though, I would be mad, and then be ashamed of myself for being mad because I knew he couldn't help it. To complicate things, when I tried to stuff my frustration by not expressing it appropriately at the time, I noticed that later it would slither out in some form of side-swiping passive aggressive behavior.

Once he was more than an hour late for a dinner party at my home. When he arrived, I, wishing to appear at least accepting, and at best saintly, gave him a kiss on the cheek, and seated him at the table with the other guests who had just finished the main course. As if watching myself in a movie and wiping my hands on my apron, I heard myself say, "Well, I guess you'll just have to go without dessert tonight."

∞

Jack S.: In a letter to his son:

Dear Jason,

Please read what I have to say very carefully. I am putting my whole heavy heart and soul into what I am about to say. I feel deep pain and frustration at not being able to help you get back your healthy life. All the past years of my trying to help have only resulted in your being angry with me for interfering with your life. My intentions have always been to help. Obviously it has not helped. I now realize there is nothing I can do. I realize I cannot "do it for you." The only one that can take control of your life is you.

I am letting go, Jason. It does not mean I have stopped caring. It means I cannot "do it for you." I will always care about you and love you. I cannot give you any money, buy cigarettes, fix your car, etc. Those are not my areas of responsibility. Giving those things only makes everything worse. I will, however, give you a ride to doctor's appointments if you call me in advance.

I miss you terribly. I respect you more than you realize. I love you more than you can imagine. Keep in touch. You are welcome to come over to visit or eat with us any time.

Love,

Dad

LET GO AND LET GOD

...training in trust...

I only let go when I was too tired to hang on any longer.

Ed F.

I never let go of anything that didn't have claw marks all over it.

Blanche D.

We reached the end of the line. We knew our emotional survival depended on it. We could honestly say we had done everything.

Betty U.

Whatever we try to control does have control over us and our life.
Melanie Beattie, author of <u>The Language of Letting Go</u>

What is the use of praying if, at the very moment of the prayer, we have so little confidence in God that we are planning our own kind of answer to our prayer?

Thomas Merton

*It is much easier to **<u>do</u>** something than to trust in God; . . .We would far rather work for God than believe in Him. Am I quite sure that God will do what I cannot do? . . . The degree of panic is the degree of the lack of personal spiritual experience.*
Oswald Chambers, from <u>My Utmost for His Highest</u>

Don't just do something— stand there!!!

-Anonymous-

LET GO AND LET GOD

The following is a reprint of a flyer which has been circulating around Twelve Step groups for many years. It describes, better than I can, what it means to "let go."

TO LET GO

To "let go" does not mean to stop caring, it means I can't do it for someone else.

To "let go" is not to cut myself off, it's the realization I can't control another.

To "let go" is not to enable, but to allow learning from natural consequences.

To "let go" is to admit powerlessness, which means the outcome is not in my hands.

To "let go" is not to try to change or blame another, it's to make the most of myself.

To "let go" is not to care for, but to care about.

To "let go" is not to fix, but to be supportive.

To "let go" is not to judge, but to allow another to be a human being.

To "let go" is not to be in the middle arranging all the outcomes, but to allow others to affect their destinies.

To "let go" is not to be protective, it's to permit another to face reality.

To "let go" is not to deny, but to accept.

To "let go" is not to nag, scold or argue, but instead to search out my own shortcomings and correct them.

To "let go" is not to adjust everything to my desires, but to take each day as it comes and cherish myself in it.

To "let go" is not to criticize and regulate anybody, but to try and become what I dream I can be.

To "let go" is not to regret the past, but to grow and live for the future.

To "let go" is to fear less and love more.

-Anonymous-

∞

When you think about it, letting go is as foreign to our human nature as jumping off a twelve story building. We know that gravity can kill us. But there are people who defy gravity—people who have overcome their fear and have been highly trained to perform the art of trapeze, high wire letting go. If you are going to save yourself and/or a loved one by "letting go," you will need training—training in transitions, timing and trust. You will discover that you don't always have to get it perfectly right. There is a safety net. But the more you practice, the more skilled you become and the greater the rewards.

By now you know you can't force yourself to let go; this is not a will power issue. Rather is it a slow process of spiritual release. We ask our Higher Power for His help to release our resistance. We want to be very patient and gentle with ourselves for being afraid to let go. Then one day when we least expect it . . . we find we have done it! Or more correctly, it has been done for us! Here are some tips to get you started:

1. Entertain the idea.
2. Observe how your attempts to control outcomes have failed.
3. Notice how much tension is in your body when you're trying so hard.
4. Don't ask, "Where are you going?" Don't say, "Don't forget to ..." Don't cover anyone else's debts.
5. Watch how things resolve themselves when you don't interfere.

6. Observe the way someone else steps in to fill the gap when you back off.
7. If, and when, you see your dependent take responsibility for a period of time, you can consider assistance with a contract and conditions.

When my son had been sober for a period of time, I agreed to let him draw money from his deceased father's trust fund for training in a skilled trade. And in my own case, my mother allowed me to come to live with her only after I accepted the reality of my mental illness and was following a course of treatment.

I think it is almost impossible to put these concepts into practice without the help of a support system, be it a Twelve Step program, supportive family groups or prayer partners. Part of our own growth and recovery from "being the strong one, going it alone and doing for others," requires that we place ourselves in an environment where we can grow spiritually, give and receive love and acceptance and be encouraged by the experience, strength and hope that is there.

∞

Karen Casey is the author of <u>Meditations</u>: <u>Each Day a New Beginning</u>. She writes, "Life is a process of letting go, letting go of conditions we can't control, letting go of people—-watching them move out of our lives, letting go of times, places, experiences. Leaving behind anyone or anyplace we have loved may sadden us, but is also provides us opportunities for growth we hadn't imagined. "These experiences push us beyond our former selves to deeper understandings of ourselves and of others."

"These experiences push us beyond our former selves to deeper understandings of ourselves and of others."

So often those experiences that sadden us or trigger pain, are the best lessons life is able to offer. Experiencing and surviving the pain that wrenches us emotionally, stretches us to new heights. Life is enriched by the pain. Our experiences with all other persons thereafter are deeper. Instead of dreading the ending of a time, the departure of a loved one, we must try to appreciate what we have gained already and know that life is fuller for it. Today will bring both goodbyes and hellos. I can meet both with gladness.

∞

Linda B.: In regard to my alcoholism, I consider my mother's "letting go" among her greatest gifts to me and they are the foundation of my over ten years' continuous sobriety today. The first occasion was when she realized that I was somehow getting drunk on diet coke (with wine added).

She asked, "Do you have a drinking problem?"

"Yes," I said.

"Well why don't you go to Alcoholics Anonymous?"

I went the next evening and went to stay. Nonetheless my path to recovery was complicated by my bipolar disorder. There were many breaks in sobriety. The last one was July 2, 1992. Mother was coming and I expected to be taken home for the weekend. (A drunk was always good for a major housecleaning, a hot meal, all the sheets changed, the broken glass swept up.) Instead of the standard routine, she handed me a letter. "Here, read this," she said.

At the end of the two-page letter—in which she said I could call her around Christmas, only if I had stayed sober—were the lines, "and therefore I resign as your mother." She left. I took a day to reflect that I'd better sober up to deal with my life since she had washed her hands of me. The Fourth of July 1992 has remained my sobriety date and my personal Independence Day ever since.

No matter how depressed or incapacitated I got thereafter (and I was hospitalized for a week in the summer of 2000), I never forgot that to take a drink would mean exile from the family. When I swirled inside a fog of negative emotions, I knew that taking a drink would close the waters of oblivion above my head irrevocably. Thanks, Mom!

∞

"I'm the oldest of three children, seven years older than my brother who committed suicide four years ago. I really miss him but I don't miss his problems."

Tanya T.: I think my Mom might have been bipolar. She certainly was depressed. I'm the oldest of three children, seven years older than my brother who committed suicide four years ago. I really miss him but I don't miss his problems. I connected with him emotionally and psychologically but my sister did not. When Mom was taking naps I felt that I needed to take responsibility for him. He got married in college and was in a band. He started drinking, weighed over 200 pounds, then quit and got a divorce. He was so gifted and very bright. He called me constantly during this time. He signed away parental rights to his two children and married for the second time in his thirties. They had a child with Cerebral Palsy. He told me he was having anxiety attacks. Through an affair, another divorce, and yet another marriage, he kept spending lots of money and calling me for more. He went from a six figure income to total disability. He kept saying, "You can see my talent. Why can't I see my own good qualities?"

For over 20 years I felt that I had to fix him. I complimented him, built up his ego. I visited him in psych wards and jail. When the police found him dead in his apartment he had taken thirty OxyContin along with all kinds of other prescription drugs.

I was diagnosed with fast cycling myself and got into AA 12-Step recovery for my drinking some years ago. Twelve Step meetings made me realize I couldn't make him better. One time I said to him, "I love you with all my heart but I can't save you and if you choose to commit suicide I will miss you."

I have learned that I can't make my gay son straight. I can't make my gifted, talented husband

> *"For over 20 years I felt that I had to fix him. I complimented him, built up his ego. I visited him in psych wards and in jail. "*

a better businessman or the kind of person who knows how to deal with finances. I am very frustrated at times. I worked very hard. I taught 31 years and sometimes I'm very angry. But I just have to let go. Sometimes I can't and things build up. And then I just have to say, "Help me, God!" I found God in AA, not in church or self-help books and I finally know that things are going to work out. I have had so much support. I work on resentments. I have that obsessive "stinking thinking." Now I work on letting go.

∞

Sally R.: In spite of all my expert nurturing and managing, my husband's blood pressure just kept getting higher (due to his drinking and smoking) and my eighteen-year-old daughter's behavior slid into a compulsive exercising/anorexic pattern. No amount of pleading, cajoling, or scheming made any difference to either one of them. In fact, their blaming and abuse of me just got worse. My head and heart ached from banging against a brick wall of denial and projection.

So I surrendered—not easily. I got down on my knees and told God I was sorry that I had tried to control other people's behavior and sought his help. I started attending an anonymous group for family members and worked the 12-Steps. I made an appointment to see a professional counselor. I had to swallow my pride as I exposed my less-than-perfect family members and my own futile attempts to fix them and make them better. My counselor asked me, "What would be the worst thing that could happen if you didn't fix them?" "Well, they might get sicker and die," I replied. "What about you?" she asked me. "I'm concerned about them," I told her. I'd never thought much about my own needs. I'd been taught that I needed to help others before myself.

My husband and daughter's diseases did get worse—for awhile. My nurturing-self wanted desperately to make them better but my counselor and my support group friends told me that I needed to let go and let God. So I prayed more and had a spiritual awakening. The presence of the Holy Spirit filled me and the words of Scripture comforted me. I discovered over time that I had received gifts of discernment and healing, not only for myself, but to be passed on to others.

∞

T. D. Jakes is a television evangelist. The following statements are excerpts from an Internet message that I received in the Spring of 2004. I assume he was preaching, when he was quoted as follows:

> *When people walk away from you: let them walk. I don't want you to try to talk another person into staying with you, loving you, calling you, caring about you, coming to see you, staying attached to you. Your destiny is never tied to anybody that left.*

> *People leave you because they are not joined to you. And if they are not joined to you, you can't make them stay. Let them go. And it doesn't mean that they are bad people. It just means that their part in the story is over. So don't keep trying to raise the dead.*

> *Let me tell you something. I've got the gift of good-bye. It's the tenth spiritual gift, I believe in good-bye. If you are holding on to something that doesn't belong to you and was never intended for your life, then you need to LET IT GO!!!*

> *If someone can't treat you right, love you back, and see your worth...*
> *LET IT GO!!!*

If you are involved in a wrong relationship or addiction ...
LET IT GO!!!

If you keep judging others to make yourself feel better...
LET IT GO!!!

If you keep trying to help someone who won't even try to help themselves...
LET IT GO!!!

If there is a particular situation that you are so used to handling yourself and God is saying, "take your hands off of it," then you need to...
LET IT GO!!!

Let the past be the past. Forget the former things. GOD is doing a new thing for you.

"The Battle is the Lord's!"

FEAR

...what if I'm afraid he'll die...

Fear, n.- dread, fright, terror, horror, panic, alarm, dismay, apprehension, mistrust, worry, disquiet, concern, angst, anguish, anxiety, cold feet, second thoughts, bugaboo, the creeps, nightmare, phobia.
                                    The Synonym Finder, Jerome I. Rodale

Everyone who dies leaves a skeleton in his closet, but the suicide leaves one in yours.
                                    Steven Levine, author of Who Dies

Surviving suicide has been another path from fear to faith.
                                    Judy Collins, author of Sanity and Grace

Fear is the razor edge of chaos.
                                    Martha Lakis

I must often remind myself, that when I am alone in my head, with only my own thoughts, I am in a dangerous neighborhood.
                                    Overheard at a 12-Step Meeting

God is our refuge and strength, an ever-present help in trouble. Therefore we will not fear though the earth give way and the mountains fall into the heart of the sea, though its waters roar and foam, and the mountains quake with their surging.
                                    Psalm 46:1-3

Peace I leave with you; my peace I give you. I do not give to you as the world gives. Do not let your hearts be troubled and do not be afraid.
                                    John 14:27

FEAR

"What is the greatest enemy of enlightenment?"
"Fear."

"And where does the fear come from?"
"Delusion."

"And what is delusion."
"To think that the flowers around you are poisonous snakes."

"How shall I attain enlightenment?"
"Open your eyes and see."

"What?"
"That there isn't a single snake around."

Dialogue between a Zen Master and his disciple.

Patricia Livingston, author of <u>This Blessed Mess,</u> chose to alter this dialogue between disciple and Master to give the glory to God. Her rewrite is as follows:

"How shall I attain enlightenment?"
"Open your eyes and see."

"What?"
"That because God is with us, no matter what happens, somehow, the snakes become flowers."

I was happy to see Livingston give a rewrite to the parable. In the 1980's, I was very much influenced by the New Age movement which incorporates strains of Buddhism in its metaphysical system. The basic tenet of Buddhism is that everything in the temporal world is an illusion. I subscribed to the philosophy that FEAR is False Evidence Appearing Real.

This was taking "Thinking makes it so," to a new delusional dimension. Another book that has impacted the New Age movement is The Course in Miracles. Here are the basics:

- People are inherently divine expressions of God; they have just forgotten who they are.
- There is no absolute truth.
- Reality is what I perceive it to be.
- If I change my perception, I can change my reality.
- There is no right or wrong, only the presence or absence of love.
- Judgment of myself and others gets in the way of unconditional love.

The light and love philosophy was very appealing. But when I became a Christian, I learned the hard way that evil is not a figment of my imagination; it is real. Indeed, there are snakes in the grass and I need to be wary and stay out of their way. During the time that I espoused a New Age philosophy it was as if I was in denial of the existence of gravity. The cure for this sort of misperception is often a good hard fall. In my case, it was a "fall into lust" and I found myself fleeing in the middle of the night from a jealous lover with a gun. The shame and degradation of that experience was a humiliating shock—just one of the painful jolts that one year later influenced me to change my mind about "Mind Science" and embrace the healing love of Jesus Christ.

It seems close to the truth to say that fear is universal to living organisms and is a God-given instinct to protect and preserve His creatures. "Flight or Fight" is an automatic mechanism designed to keep us alive long enough to reproduce ourselves. We are human. We fear pain and death. We, who are codependents, fear being out of control. We fear there is something wrong with us. Some of us fear God. The problem faced by human beings living today is that the adrenalin rush, which kept our primitive ancestors alive, is not effective in dealing with our contemporary environment. We are rarely faced with real snakes, but our minds and bodies still act as if we do. It is emotional stress we face. Increased adrenalin, with no place to go, is killing us.

Having no fear is not a healthy situation either. Fear, like guilt, can be both constructive and destructive. Franklin Delano Roosevelt, the 32nd President of the United States, told the American public at the onset of World War II: "The only thing we have to fear is fear itself." He was acknowledging the reality of fear and exhorting the nation not to be immobilized by it. The solution is not to pretend that the snakes are flowers, but to arm ourselves with physical, emotional and spiritual weapons for protection.

If you are in a relationship with a person who has a mental illness or an addiction, you know how vulnerable they are to their own poor choices, and to others who would take advantage of them, knowingly or unknowingly. If you are reading this book, it is likely that you know you cannot give them the protection they need. Enablers, fixers and controllers who maintain their action-oriented "strong one" role may never have had to stop short and confront their fears. Some of us are so afraid of our loved one's dying that we are not able to live our own lives.

∞

Lorraine P.: While I slept, I tried to rescue both my husband and my daughter. I had nightmares about my husband having a heart attack or another disabling stroke. I dreamt that my daughter was drowning at sea while I tried to run into the water to save her but my feet couldn't move. I developed a condition called irritable bowel syndrome. Frequent bladder infections reminded me that my body suffered from buried emotions of fear, anxiety, and anger.

∞

Retired addiction therapist, Joann Comer reminds us that we cannot truly discuss the emotion of fear without looking at its emotional partner, anger. Comer says, "Anger is rampant in the presence of alcohol or other drug abuse. The abuser is angry, most of all with him or herself for violating, over and over, his or her own values." She notes that the anger is hard to live with because it can lead to more substance abuse and because it is usually turned on the family. This leads to a "familyful" of anger.

The mental illness or addiction of one family member is likely to have far reaching emotional consequences for everyone in the family. Anger leads to blame. Blame leads to shame, discouragement, disappointment, fatigue, loss and hopelessness. The result is emotional shut down and the building of defenses such as coldness, super-responsibility, martyrdom and manipulation. Many people, who grew up in such a family, have said that what they knew of love they learned from their alcoholic/ drug-abusing parent because, at least when they weren't using, they were "there" for them. The caregiver parent seldom has much left over to give.

So what can be done to deal with anger? The first step is to become aware and learn that anger is, primarily, a secondary emotion. Like an iceberg rising above the water, the primary mass is under the surface and must be dealt with to prevent the total wreckage of a relationship. When this is understood, the anger can be dealt with in healthier ways. As an example, let's suppose your teenage son has left the car in front of the house overnight with the keys in the ignition and the doors unlocked. Your first reaction is probably going to be anger. You can stomp back into the house and shout about his thoughtlessness and irresponsibility, or you can tell him that you your heart just sank into your shoes when because you discovered that your only means of getting to work was put at risk needlessly and you just feel sick when you discovered it. If you don't put the other person on the defensive, they are more likely to be able to see the situation from your perspective as well as their own.

∞

During the last twenty years I have spoken to hundreds of people, usually family members who were concerned about their relative's substance abuse, mood disorders and violent or self-destructive behavior. They focused on poor grades, surly attitudes, poor money management, family disruptions, lack of insight and blaming. What they seemed to be reluctant to discuss was the fear that their loved one might die and they would feel responsible. It was as if talking about it might make it more likely to actually happen.

Personally, I found that I was unable to break my enabling pattern until I acknowledged my fear that my son might die. One of my most effective support groups reinforced that, "I didn't cause it. I can't cure it." It was clear that I couldn't keep him alive; the next best thing was to stop being vulnerable to the very sort of manipulation and deception that addicts so skillfully use to maintain their self-destructive lifestyles.

And I have also experienced first hand, either the blessing or the curse, (however you care to look at it), of having one of the things I most feared come to pass. What middle-aged, single woman hasn't been afraid of becoming a bag lady?   I never believed that in a few short years, undiagnosed and untreated mental illness could take me from health and prosperity to

> *"Personally, I found that I was unable to break my enabling pattern until I acknowledged my fear that my son might die."*

psychosis, bankruptcy and homelessness. At the height of my mania I did not jump over Niagara Falls, but I did have the delusions of grandeur that caused me to take the sort of death-defying financial risks and that plunged me into financial ruin. The age of 57 is a bit late in life to be wiped out!! But God came through after all! The crisis of consequences woke me up to the need for help.

My illness and recovery have given me a whole new lease on life. If I had not been indigent, I would not have qualified for "free to me" psychiatric supervision, therapy, medication, case management and even a short term stay in a crisis residential unit. Publicly funded welfare truly "fared well" for me. My mother offered to let me live with her temporarily and that was a healing experience for both of us. Even in the midst of such devastation, my faith was far greater than my fear.

But even under excellent professional medical care, I faced major challenges. Hoping to get back into my right mind, I consented to treatment with the use of three psychotropic drugs. I was not prepared that the cure might feel worse than the disease. These medications, which I was counting on to restore me to sanity, had mind-altering side effects. I was used to a hyperactive brain, plenty of energy, creative thoughts. This was me, alive! The drugs, designed to slow me down, made me feel that my identity had been stripped away. I feared I

> *"I was used to a hyperactive brain, plenty of energy, creative thoughts. This was me, alive!"*

would never function as an intelligent adult again. I now knew, from personal experience, why others stop taking their medications. But I was fortunate to have three factors in my favor which helped me get through the difficult transition from psychosis to balance. My bottom was so low that I surrendered to the wisdom of my psychiatrist. He continued to reassure me that, "this too would pass." I believed him when he said I would adjust and that some medications would be eliminated once I stabilized. I was treatment compliant because I put myself there, not because some one else thought it would be a good idea. And finally, I trusted that God had a fail-safe insurance plan that could cover the inevitable mess ups of human error.

Faith and prayer are effective remedies for fear but there are other mind-altering strategies as well. Most phobia clinics teach people how to live more comfortably with their fears, not eliminate them entirely. But they first must face the fear. For example, some of us fly in airplanes often and comfortably; some of us fly with white knuckles. Some of us will never get in an airplane. The difference is in the way we think about it. Imagine yourself walking across a board lying flat on the ground in your backyard. It is three feet wide and twenty feet long. An easy stroll, right?

Now imagine that the same board is fifteen feet off the ground. This time it's not such a casual stretch. Same task, different perception.

Many of us have overcome situations that used to paralyze us. What happened to my fear of driving on the freeway? What happened to your fear of skiing as you now enjoy the thrill of descending the slopes? Did it magically disappear? Did you fight it? Lean into it? Feel it and do it anyway?

∞

An article in the January 20, 2003 issue of <u>Time Magazine</u> reported that suicide is the second leading cause of death among young people. Suicide threats must be taken seriously. But those of us who deal with chemically dependent persons need also be aware that addicts often manipulate parents, therapists and caregivers with threats of suicide to keep them locked into enabling and taking responsibility for the dependent's problems.

It will help reduce the fear that your loved one will self-destruct when you begin to talk about it with that person and with others. It can be a simple, non-accusatory, non-manipulative dialogue of care and concern. By openly acknowledging suicide potential, you have a better chance of investigating its gravity and intention, opening the door to communication and diffusing it as a possible manipulative technique. You demonstrate courage when you say, "It's OK to talk about suicidal feelings. You know how much we care about you. You appear very depressed about your life. Have you been thinking about suicide? Some people consider it when life becomes too painful. I want you to know there is help available to you if you want it. I will be there for you."

∞

Folksinger, Judy Collins wrote about her son's death in <u>Sanity and Grace</u>. She said, "I had tried to do everything I could do to help my son, but Clark was an adult. He was thirty-three. He was a man, a father, and a husband. I couldn't fight Clark's demons, and he fought them and lost. Or won, depending on your definition of faith. As my own guilt began to subside and I heard the voices of others who had walked the path I was on, I began to realize that my son's suicide was a choice I had to honor, rather than take as an attempt on my own life, an unacceptable act that tore my heart apart. I began to see that this is just another path to acceptance and surrender. When

I began to accept this terrible action as my son's path and his destiny, I began to forgive him and myself and to find a way out of the dark place."

∞

Mary Ann Q.: I am a social worker. When my daughter was in her junior year of college, she went through a very confusing time. She was overloaded with work, unsure about her future, unhappy in love and scared to death of failing an up-coming math equivalency exam. She went to a mental health clinic on campus. She called me to say she was having a nervous breakdown and wanted to drop out of school. She told me that the counselor had told her depression was a result of being raised in a dysfunctional family. She said if life was going to be this painful, she didn't think she wanted to continue living it.

I had a choice about how to think about this situation. I could view her as clinically depressed, but was reluctant to label her as "sick," for fear that she would see herself that way. I could see it as a transitional stage of developmental growing pains. Or I could see her condition as a cop-out, just a way to get out of a tough situation. I wondered if she had some unfinished business with me before she could move on to adult independence. I did not want to be defensive about my role in her problems. I hoped I had the ability to stand by her during this troubled time and be a supportive partner. I knew she was asking me for help. And I wanted to empower her to help herself towards a healthy responsible life.

When she came home I asked her what she needed. Hospitalized psychiatric treatment? Out-patient therapy with a counselor? A rest? Or a change of activity? I confronted the suicide issue directly and she reassured me that that was not in her mind. She decided she wanted to be relieved of the pressure of school and decided to get a job and get some counseling. She asked me to go with her. I agreed and also let her pay for the part of her therapy which was not covered by my insurance. In three months decided that living at home and working was not what she wanted, and she went back to school in the spring quarter. She graduated from college, had a career and today is a happily married   mother of three beautiful children!

I think I grew personally and professionally in this experience too. I realized that much of my early parenting was accompanied by guilt and fear. I suspect that I inherited that pattern from my own mother.

∞

How in heaven's name can "fear of the Lord" help us be less fearful? "Fear the Lord," is repeated in The Holy Bible just as often as 'Fear not!" But I think it has caused a lot of people to close the Good Book altogether, because they do not want to serve an angry, punitive God. So perhaps we would benefit from a broadened understanding of the God of the Old Testament if we translate "fear" into "respect." Consider for example the awesome power of the ocean. I lived in North County San Diego for four years. During that time I spent a lot of time in the water. I am not a surfer, but I heard enough hard-core surfer stories to develop a healthy respect for the waves and currents. In order to be safe, I had to learn as much as I could about the nature of this wonderful element. Regard for power is wise.

> *The fear of the Lord is the beginning of knowledge,*
> *But fools despise wisdom and discipline.*
>
> Proverbs 1:7

Some people with mental illness have no fear. They behave as if they have superhuman powers. The same can often be said of people who are on Ecstasy, LSD or methamphetamines. Alcohol can make anyone foolish. Therefore, some fear, like some guilt, is healthy. Likewise, "fear of the Lord," can remind us of His sovereignty and give us comfort when our own resources are dried up.

GUILT
...red flag or black dog...

Guilt, n. - remorse, regret, contrition, contriteness, compunction, sorrow, penitence, repentance, self-reproach, self-accusation, self-condemnation, self-reproof.

The Synonym Finder, Jerome I. Rodale

In most cases, those who intend to kill themselves do just that, and therapy, as well as other means of support, seldom prevents a determined individual from taking his own life if he determines to do so. Though often useful, professional help is no guarantee against suicide.

George Stone, author of Suicide and Attempted Suicide

Survivors of suicide are routinely implicated and may feel guilty. They tend in retrospect to check out everything they ever said or did with regard to the suicide. You hear it all the time. "He called. I didn't call him back. I feel so guilty! I didn't answer the letter, I should have known. He looked so happy, how could I have known?" All survivors are suspect.

Judy Collins, author of Sanity and Grace

Guilt is the gift that keeps on giving.

Columnist Erma Bombeck

Therefore, there is now no condemnation for those who are in Christ Jesus, because through Christ Jesus the law of the Spirit of life set me free from the law of sin and death.

Romans 8:1-2

GUILT

Do you agree that guilt is a universal emotion in our culture and the absence of it is seen as a pathological abnormality?   Do you think guilt is constructive or destructive?

Bob Mandel, author of <u>Open Heart Therapy,</u> wrote:

> *Guilt is the Mafia of the mind. It is a protection plan we sell ourselves in order to avoid anticipated punishment. All guilt is masochistic . . . Guilt is based on the illusion that pain is redemption rather than innocence. Guilt makes martyrs think they are saints. Guilt is the godfather masquerading as God . . . The antidote is to see that we create our own pain and pleasure as do others. Forgiveness frees us from guilt. We must first forgive ourselves for pretending to be guilty.*

When I wrote <u>Recovery from Rescuing</u>, Mandel's ideas seemed very attractive to me, as they would to anyone who had been beating herself up with "could have, should have, would have's" all her life. But later I discovered that, like a counterfeit hundred dollar bill, it turned out to be deceptive: a fake that seduced me with its patina of truth. There are many such "look good, feel good, sound good" philosophies that just don't hold up to the test of life and death. Try passing some counterfeit money. Sooner or later some bank teller will deliver it back to the holder with the message that it is worthless.

Over the years my understanding of, and my relationship with, my Higher Power has changed. A spiritual evolution is the way I think of it. Maybe I was in the spiritual ball park, but kind of "out in left field," for awhile. The events that got me closer to home plate were not pleasant. I had to face my human limitations instead of embrace my goddess grandiosity. I saw myself as I really am: human, not divine. I realized I did not have the power to forgive myself or will myself into unconditional love. I wanted those qualities but knew I needed help.

Today I prefer to write about guilt from a Christian perspective because, for me, it is the truth. Now, the source of my understanding about guilt comes from the Scriptures. I begin with the premise that no one is truly innocent. We are not even born innocent. All are guilty by virtue of our human nature.

> *This righteousness from God comes through faith in Jesus Christ to all who believe. There is no difference for all have sinned and fall short of the glory of God, and are justified freely by his grace through the redemption that came by Christ Jesus. God presented him as a sacrifice of atonement, through faith in his blood.*
>
> Romans 3:22-25

∞

Gwen Shamblin, the founder and teacher of Weigh Down, a Christian weight loss program tells us that there are two kinds of guilt: real guilt and false guilt. To further clarify the difference, let's label real guilt as Red Flag Guilt and false guilt as "The Black Dog." Winston Churchill referred to his long-standing clinical depression as "the black dog." False guilt is an oppressive weight that seems like it will never go away. It slinks around, trying to take cover from being exposed to the light, but its presence is still ominous. It is important to recognize that unrealistic guilt is a sign of depression as well.

Shamblin notes that in Jesus' day, the Pharisees, with their hypocritical legalism, were always placing guilt on the Jews to keep them under control. The oppression was almost too much to bear. This form of hierarchal authoritative guilt makes God's children vulnerable to false guilt and manipulation. Many of us can think of instances in which we were jockeyed around by our siblings, children, parents or spouses because they knew which guilt buttons to push in us in order to get what they wanted. And at the same time, who among us hasn't used guilt as leverage in a relationship negotiation. If you feel guilty about a divorce, job pressures, the way you brought up your children, you may be setting yourself up as your own Pharisee. Watch out that "The Black Dog," false guilt, doesn't cause your children or others to manipulate you into enabling behaviors. You do not need to cover their mistakes. Jesus came to set us free from that bondage of Pharisaic false guilt.

It is especially important for "people pleasers" to discriminate between false guilt and real guilt. If we have trouble distinguishing between the two, anything or anybody can make us feel guilty. Ask yourself, your Higher Power and other people: "Are you dealing with the Red Flag or being dealt a dirty hand by the Black Dog?"

Red Flag guilt is real and constructive. Some call it conscience. It can be described as the still small, gentle, but unrelenting, voice of God. He wants to lead each of us into a closer relationship with Him and His plan for our life. "The Lord is my shepherd," the Bible tells us. He is loving and forgiving, but He is also a righteous God who wants us to mature. A shepherd must be both vigilant and clever, for it is no secret that sheep are pretty aimless and not very smart about staying on a path of righteousness. So conscience is one of the gentler tools that keeps us on the straight and narrow. Unlike the rod and staff which give a somewhat stronger message, the Red Flag of guilt is just a road sign that assists us in following the Shepherd. When we are blind or disobedient to the signal because we think it is a form of intimidation, i.e. the Godfather, instead of God, we are likely to get lost or fall into a deep crevice.

A friend confided to me recently that she is plagued with guilt because she thinks she should be encouraging her mentally ill son to be more independent. He is in his forties and has lived with her for a long time. She said, "It is simply too frightening for me not to keep track of what's going on with him. At the same time, I'm not getting any younger and I wonder what will happen when I'm not there to be the caretaker." She is not alone is this ambivalence. Of course, there are no easy answers but it is helpful to delineate self-serving motives from God-serving motives.

$$\infty$$

Shirley K.: Neither my bridge guests nor I will ever forget the winter evening in 1984 when my estranged, drug-addicted son showed up at the front door late in the evening. I turned him away with a $10.00 bill and a list of emergency shelter and addiction treatment agency phone numbers. This was not people-pleasing behavior. My friends were shocked. What they did not know was that the last time I let him come home because I felt sorry about his situation and guilty about my parenting, he had stolen a diamond ring out of my jewelry box.

$$\infty$$

In Sanity and Grace, Judy Collins describes her initial grief after her son committed suicide. "I was living by a thread, feeling sorrow, and despair. And contrary to what I knew was logical, I felt guilt. But a few days later,

Joan Rivers called to connect with me, another survivor. Her husband had taken his own life and she had been contacted by mutual friends about Clark's death. Joan was comforting and generous and her personal talks with me, by phone and in person, sometimes from the backstage dressing rooms of her shows in cities around the country . . . her voice often got me through another night. There were many other supportive, wise friends who had lost children, husbands, friends and parents. They all said that there are no guilts in suicide. I believed them even though I felt too weak to walk or even think straight. I wept, knowing they were right, must be right."

∞

Talia S.: After last week I realize I have to make some changes in the way I handle my sister's illness. I have been trying for years to make it better, volunteering to take the kids, giving money to the family when things got rehab she got mad, of course and said her husband was against that. He thinks that she just needs to get back to work. I look back and see the pattern of her being mean to me and others, blaming me for the difficulties in our relationship and I'm sick of that. For this week I have made progress. I didn't call to find out how she's doing, I didn't offer to help. I am backing off.

"I just had to say no. And I feel so guilty."

She has had so much difficulty keeping relationships and she wants to be part of my social circle and I can't do that anymore. Even though I've tried, in the past, to include her. She called and asked me if I would put in a word with my friend's husband about getting her a job. With her depression untreated right now and her inability to hold the last four jobs in two years, I just had to say no. And I feel so guilty. Part of me wants to help to keep doing what I've been doing and the other part knows I just have to let go.

∞

Patsy Q.: When our adopted son was diagnosed with developmental disabilities we, as parents, felt dismayed. One doctor told us his "wires are crossed." I was a teacher. He was difficult when he was young; he couldn't focus. He was hyperactive, always up on top of everything. Once he fell out of a tree but wasn't hurt. He grew to be a sweet child, but his charming innocence made him vulnerable.

The doctor said, "you have to be understanding and accepting." We mourned, right away, the fantasy of what we hoped he could be. We got help and that has enabled us to accept what can't be changed and work to change the things we can.

Now he is thirty one. He is in a sheltered workshop. We support him. He has a live-in girlfriend and we help her too. We had to take his license away because he couldn't focus. He could do more, others say. But he steals and I want to protect him from places and situations that would open up his impulsivity. He's not a criminal. There are

"I feel guilt, because I always think I'm not doing enough."

always a lot of "whoops" he can't see. The onus seems to be on me. In spite of therapy, I don't always handle it very well. I feel guilt, because I always think I'm not doing enough. I expected to be the perfect parent.

DUTY, OBLIGATION AND RESPONSIBILITY

...love or legalism...

Responsibility, n. - accountability, liability, duty, obligation, onus, burden, charge, care, custody, jurisdiction, office, trust, task, part, role, fault, guilt, blame, culpability, reprehensibleness

                              The Synonym Finder, Jerome I. Rodale

You don't have to do anything. The more you do, the worse it gets. All you have to do is understand.

                              Anthony deMello, S.J.

There is no responsibility on you for the work; the only responsibility you have is to keep in living constant touch with God and to see that you allow nothing to hinder your co-operation with Him.

                    Oswald Chambers, from My Utmost for His Highest

People who tend to make things happen, often need to learn to let things happen and people who like to let things happen, often need to learn to make things happen.

                              -Anonymous-

If you knew how often I say to myself: to hell with everything; to hell with everybody, I've done my share, let the others do theirs now. Enough, enough, enough!

                    Golda Meir, former Prime Minister of Israel

DUTY, OBLIGATION
AND RESPONSILIBITY

It is written in Genesis 4:2-5:

> *Now Abel kept flocks, and Cain worked the soil. In the course of time Cain brought some of the fruits of the soil as an offering to the Lord. But Abel brought fat portions from some of the firstborn of his flock. The Lord looked with favor on Abel and his offering, but on Cain and his offering he did not look with favor.*

One of the differences between the Old Testament and the New Testament is the concept of legalism or the emphasis on "The Law." If you are not a student of Scripture, you may wonder why God rejected Cain's sacrifice and accepted that of Abel, since outwardly both appeared to meet the legal requirements. The answer is that God knew the motive of each man's heart. Cain was giving grudgingly, simply going through the motions of duty and obligation to the law; Abel loved God and wished to give his gift out of a grateful heart, not because it was required. The purpose of this chapter is to help us decipher the motives of our hearts for the actions we take.

For some, the word "responsibility" conjures up feelings of guilt and punishment. We may remember a disapproving parent standing over the broken cookie jar saying, "Who's responsible for this?" Thus I was in great turmoil when my best efforts could not keep my accident-prone son safe and secure. And I felt powerless when his aggressive, violent behavior at home threatened his sisters' mental and physical health. What was my responsibility in this situation? Was it necessary for me to abdicate my role as his mother because I couldn't fulfill my duties, obligations and responsibilities? Did all of this happen because I didn't love him enough?

Discussing her son's death by suicide, Judy Collins said, "I know from walking the grid of looking at every fact about my son's death, that anyone who saw the facts for what they were, would have known that my son was on the veritable edge of completing the act of suicide for months before his death. He tried, and failed, and tried again . . . I also know that although he blamed others for most of his mood of the day, no one is responsible for his death other than himself . . . Suicide, though it may have many causes is often the ultimate third finger salute, the clutched fingers under the chin, fist against the forearm and curse to anyone near enough to get the message."

∞

Susan L.: My daughter taught me the meaning of despair. I thought I understood it, but I really didn't. I love my daughter. And she was such a good girl. Even-tempered, funny, loving and very intelligent. She began reading classic literature in the fourth grade and by the time she reached high school, she was in the top 10 out of 600 students in her grade. She was perfect. And she developed a disorder we later learned was common in "perfect" children.

My daughter entered puberty at age seventeen. At the same time, she began self-injuring. Then she began a speedy downward slide into severe depression. Her senior year was a bizarre contrast for us as we attended program after program honoring her achievements while at home we were tearing her room apart daily searching for picket knives and razor blades. At one point she had over 500 fresh cuts on each leg. They were a bloody, scarred, scabby mess—but she had counted every cut. They were neat, in even rows of five, Thin, red musical staffs etched on her body forever.

I yelled, I cried, I begged. I snooped through her journals, read things I never should have seen. I spent hours researching self-injury on the internet. Our library had little information except the cursory copy of "Reviving Ophelia." It didn't really help. In two months we went from a normal family to a freakish, dysfunctional group of people trying to coexist under one roof.

> *"I will admit I was manic in my efforts to protect this child from herself."*

Of course we had her in therapy immediately. The therapist told us that the cutting wasn't the big deal, only the symptom. The depression was the much more serious issue. Then I found out that she had been taking Motrin 40-70-200 at a time. She described how they made her feel. Then we knew she had a pain in her soul that massive doses couldn't assuage. The therapist told us she fantasized about killing herself. That's when I learned despair. No matter what I did—and I will admit I was manic in my efforts to protect this child from herself, I finally realized I couldn't save her. It racked my gut with pain. I could feel it in my bones. I wished I could die myself before she did, so I wouldn't feel the loss I knew was inevitable.

She graduated from high school. We gave her a grand party. Of the over one hundred people at the house, only we, and my sister, knew of her secret torment. And no one knew my husband and I were going to commit her to a hospital for treatment the next day. The therapist had warned us that our daughter was likely to see graduation as the best time to end her life. With our permission the therapist made the arrangements.

The first hospitalization was only the beginning. Over the next year she was readmitted twice for suicide attempts, endured eighteen medication changes and was on the brink of electroconvulsive treatment. We had given up. We sent her to my husband's sister's house in New York believing she would die there and not in the same house with our son.

To our amazement she called after six weeks and said the terrorizing visions were going away, she was not going to die and wanted to come home. The doctors tell us that she will always need to be on medications, and that is fine with us. Today she functions as if most of that trauma didn't ever happen. She's still a little "brainiac"—in an accelerated master's degree program at the University of Michigan, holds down a responsible job and is completing a difficult internship. All of our relationships are rock solid. Her dad, brother and I love her as much, and perhaps more than before, knowing how close we came to losing her.

I truly believe that if she had continued to live under our roof during the rock bottom of the depression—I'm sure she would not be with us today. I was trying too hard to save her from herself and that may have pushed her farther and farther away. Once she became responsible for her own life, I think she realized that it was a partnership between her and her doctor that would save her—that is where she would find the means to stop the pain that was driving her to death. We couldn't do it for her, as much as I wanted to. It was all her, with the miracle of modern science and a competent physician as a guide!

∞

Those of us, who have faced such life and death circumstances with our loved ones, have had to redefine the concepts of duty, obligation and responsibility in terms of "our ability to respond." This seems to help eliminate some of the self-judgment and clarify the issues. For me the "ability to respond" means that when I am in a crisis, my responsibility is to see it as a spiritual opportunity. I want to see the conflict from God's perspective. I want to avoid hasty manipulation of other people or outer circumstances. When I am given the grace to do it, I pray, journal, seek wise and trustworthy counsel. Then I am grateful for the ability to be more, not less, responsive to the situation and the other people in it.

How would you define "over responsibility?" I define it as "playing God." As several of our testimonies have indicated, this tendency can be addictive because there are so many rewards for it, at home and at work. There is nothing wrong with taking on the weight of the world unless the burden immobilizes you. We all know many "saints" who run ministries, non-profits and yes, even large corporations. And they have the heart for it!! Those of us with the "fix it fixation" must continuously ask ourselves, if we are operating under the banner of legalism or love. I want to be sure I'm not taking on a "God Job."

When my son was released from jail on strict probation last year for substance abuse violations, a friend of mine said, "And he's got all of your expertise in recovery to help him." "Not unless he asks for it," said I. I learned over many years of trying to give him the benefit of my good ideas that it would be far better for everyone concerned if department social workers, court appointed psychiatrist and urine police were monitoring his "rehabilitation." I'm so very happy to be retired from that job!

∞

Anthony deMello, a Jesuit priest who lived in India was the author of five best selling books. His friends said he taught people how to pray, how to enjoy life and how to "wake up and live." Students remember that one of the tasks he considered most important was to "improve God's reputation on earth." On the topic of responsibility he wrote:

And that's all right. To say no to people—-that's wonderful; that's part of waking up. Part of waking up is that you live your life as you see fit. And understand: That is not selfish. The selfish thing is to demand that someone else live their life as YOU see fit. That's selfish. It is not selfish to live your life as you see fit. The selfishness lies in demanding that someone else live their life to suit your tastes, or your pride, or your profit, or your pleasure. That is truly selfish. So I'll protect myself. I won't feel obligated to be with you; I won't feel obligated to say yes to you. If I find your company pleasant, then I'll enjoy it without clinging to it. But I no longer avoid you because of any negative feelings you create in me. You don't have that power anymore.

∞

Many years ago, I was upset about my nineteen-year-old daughter's financial problems. I offered her the benefit of my experience. She didn't take my advice and resented my interference. I realized that I felt guilty and responsible for her plight. I felt that if I had been a better mother, I would have taught her more about money management and she wouldn't be in this situation.   In feeling that I was responsible for her irresponsibility, the next step was to wonder if I "should" volunteer to pay her debts and give her a fresh start!   Perhaps you have done that, too? Maybe more than once. In this situation, my heightened sense of responsibility was a mask for guilt.

Maybe you have been picking up the pieces of other people's bad decisions so they didn't have to feel the pain. Maybe it is our own pain we are really trying to alleviate. It is not wrong to interfere or right to let go. Each situation is unique. Our ability to respond with happy results for all is enhanced by our willingness to be aware of the whole picture—our patterns, our guilt, our perception of responsibility.

When my oldest daughter was away at college, I had a long drive up north to see her. I had been looking forward to a nice long bath in the motel room but she wanted me to go shopping right away.   I nobly sacrificed my desire to accommodate hers. While we were pushing the cart around, she asked, "How come you're not being very nice to me?"   I thought I was being "nice" by meeting her request.   Later, I saw that my daughter was giving me an opportunity to get honest. She picked up on the "oh, so subtle" truth: underneath my compliant behavior, I really didn't want to be pushing a cart around K Mart. I learned that when I am present out of a sense of guilt, duty or obligation, I am participating in a business deal, not an act of generosity.

Here are some tips that can help us improve our "ability to respond."

1. Responsibility means I will not make myself a victim. I will not blame anyone else for anything I do or don't do, any condition I have or don't have, any emotion that hurts. I know that the only way out of my victim position is to "own my own stuff." Eleanor Roosevelt said, "No one can offend me without my permission."

2. Responsibility means I will not make myself the villain. I will observe what is going on, be aware of my part in it and avoid self- condemnation. I will learn from my mistakes.

3. I will remember that. I can not always control what happens to me, but I can control how I react to it.

∞

Frederick Rimpoche, a musician and poet who has experienced bipolar disorder, wrote, "When I was first hospitalized I began to feel, right in the marrow of my bones, that it was incumbent upon me to literally bear the weight of the world. I was one thought shy of thinking that I was Christ himself."

Rimpoche says that he started to obsess about all that was wrong in the world, like war, racism, child abuse, spousal violence, drug additions. He believes that the force underlying these delusions is the same force that motivated Christ himself, that of love for everyone and everything in the world. He describes it as a "love so intense that you'd be willing to undergo extreme physical discomfort on the material plane, such as crucifixion, or extreme psychological discomfort on a, shall we say, metaphysical plane, such as the onset of mental illness itself."

The writer says he developed two rationales that broke the cycle of delusions, each from a different religious tradition. Raised as a Christian, he spoke to himself as he entered the hospital:

> *So you think you might be the Son of God. If that is true then you must be at the center of the second coming. If this is the second coming, then remember. . . you have already been crucified, descended into hell, and rose again three days later for the Glory of the Resurrection. You already defeated death and all sin in every form. Why do you think you need to do it AGAIN?!?*

In this "aha!" epiphany, Rimpoche woke up on the psychiatric unit feeling a great sense of relief. "Oh thank God, I'm not Jesus Christ. He already paid the price and all I have to do is put my full faith and life into His hands and I'm saved." Frederick notes that because his illness is repetitive, he will use this thought process continually to chip away at the rock of his pathology until it all becomes a "pile of harmless little pebbles that I can step over, or around, easily."

From the Buddhist tradition, which centers on the concept of the "oneness of all creatures and creation," Rimpoche reminds himself that it is not really just one person's responsibility to bear the weight of the world—it is everyone's responsibility. And if everyone sees that and lives accordingly, each individual's burden is much lighter and far more bearable. Frederick Rimpoche observes, "In a way, mentally ill people, who view themselves as potential saviors, may not be too far off the mark—it's just that everybody else has to catch up with them so we can all do this thing together!"

LOVE

...addictive or authentic...

Love, n., v.t. - (1) a profoundly tender, passionate affection for a person of the opposite sex (2) a feeling of warm personal attachment or deep affection as for a parent, child or friend (3) affectionate concern for the well-being of others (4) deep and enduring emotional regard (5) the charity of the creator, reverence towards God . . .

Random House Dictionary of the English Language

"What is love?"
"The total absence of fear," said the Master.

"What is it we fear?"
"Love," said the Master.

Anthony deMello, SJ

I can't live without you. I can't make it on my own. All the hard times are worth the good times. I will be here forever, no matter what happens. I can't get enough of your lovin'.

Selected lyrics from country music

Love is patient, love is kind. It does not envy, it does not boast, it is not proud. It is not rude, it is not self-seeking, it is not easily angered, it keeps no record of wrongs. Love does not delight in evil but rejoices with the truth. It always protects, always trust, always hopes, always perseveres.

I Corinthians 13: 4-6

My love life is finally so wonderful that I'm ready for someone else to join me in it.

Jeff Cavanaugh

Tough love is the highest sense of loyalty.

William Guy, M.D

LOVE

There seems to be much confusion about what love is and what love isn't, especially in our culture. Perhaps it's because our language doesn't distinguish between the myriad forms of feeling and/or behavior we call "love." And in spite of all that has been written, it is still a mystery. It can be addictive, authentic, tough, protective, paternal, charitable, sacrificial, and/or self-nurturing. The Greeks differentiated "Eros," erotic, sexual love (the transitory "falling in love" phenomenon) from "philios," brotherly love, and love of friends. "Agape" is the Greek word that defines Christ-like, selfless love: loyal, benevolent, with primary concern for the well-being of another. From a spiritual perspective this is love based on the deliberate choice of the lover, rather than the worthiness of the one loved, as in the sacrificial love of God for His creatures. By contrast, "Eros" is love that arises out of our needs. It is the part of us that looks for love on the outside. It is self-centered and self-suffering. Erotic love is all about "how you make me FEEL!" It believes that there is not enough love to go around. It fears that love will go away. It holds on. It is jealous, manipulative, judgmental and self-critical. It is the love that turns itself on and off.

I am not very fond of the word "codependency." Even fifteen years ago, when the word and the subject dominated therapy sessions and television talk shows, it was confusing to many. Now, it just seems cliché and passé. Interesting, isn't it, that the word "codependency" is not listed in either the <u>Miriam Webster Dictionary</u> or the <u>Random House Dictionary of the English Language.</u> Because I wanted to discuss the concept of addictive love in this chapter, I wanted to find a more substantive word for it. A friend of mine once talked about "sticky love" to describe the excessive emotional attachment to one person. The word "enmeshment" is defined as *"to catch or entangle in."* This suggests bondage, as opposed to boundaries, in relationships. I think that gets to the heart of the difference between "addictive" and "authentic" love.

The <u>Woman's Study Bible</u> describes enmeshment or addictive love as, "the quest to meet needs."

The term codependency with its diverse definitions was coined in the context of treating alcoholism. However, it has evolved to mean a compulsion to rescue or control others by fixing their problems. Generally codependency emanates from unmet or blocked God-given needs, such as love, acceptance, and security in primary relationships as with parent, spouse or child.

More frequently codependency occurs in relationships with a dysfunctional person, resulting in a denial of the severity of the problem in the relationship, a heightened sense of responsibility and an environment of controlling or being controlled by others. It nearly always produces a keen sense of guilt or shame, hurt, anger and loneliness in a complex and desperate quest to avoid abandonment. Ultimately, this need for acceptance can only be filled by God alone. His unconditional love prepares the codependent to move toward complete healing.

Irene Matiatos, Ph.D., a licensed psychologist in New York, says that codependent people are some of the nicest people you could ever know. She says they never refuse to do a favor; they understand other people and know how to make them feel good. And that is all a good thing, UNLESS the giving is all one sided and hurts the giver. Dr. Matiatos explains that many of these individuals grew up in a home where they were expected to care for others rather than get their own needs met. The natural enmeshment with the parent is distorted and the child loses the care freeness of childhood. Trained to worry youngsters develop the art of anticipating the needs of the other person as survival skills. Mastering them becomes a life and death situation for a child. Thus, as adults, these individuals are starved for approval, have little self respect, fear abandonment and are vulnerable to abuse. They are unaware of their motives and they believe that to discontinue their sacrificial behavior would be disloyal and downright dangerous! Codependent people rarely realize how angry they are because they were trained to suppress it. Thus the rage is internalized and converted into hypersensitivity, obsession to control, hyperactivity, depression, addictions and severe self-criticism.

∞

In Please Don't Say You Need Me: Biblical Answers for Codependency, author Jan Silvious, writing specifically for Christians, defines codependency as a relationship between two people who allow one another's behavior to profoundly affect each other. She observes that Christians are not exempt from the captivity of their own unmet physical, emotional and spiritual needs and the compulsion to protect the feelings of the dependent member. She notes irony in the fact that the very people who support abstinence from alcohol and drugs, because of their addictive nature, are blind to the mind-altering, powerful and ungodly addiction to other people. She writes, "Somehow it seems almost Christ-like to be in a relationship that requires total absorption, devotion and sacrifice—especially when one feels so unworthy." She calls it "suffering from sin," because such individuals are under the influence of idolatry. Webster's Dictionary defines an "idol" as an image, representation or symbol of a deity made or consecrated as an object of worship...the object of excessive attachment, admiration, or veneration. So when the Lord says no idols, He means nothing, or no one else, should be the object of excessive attachments.

In conclusion, it is critical for all of us to see how destructive and damaging codependent behavior is. The bottom line is that enablers NEED their child, client, parent, friend or spouse to STAY sick, so they have someone to care for. It is the only way they know how to prop up their self-esteem.

$$\infty$$

In contrast to "addictive love," or enabling behavior and the enmeshment that masquerades as altruism, "authentic love" is honest, tough and corrective, charitable and self-nurturing. It does not walk on egg shells, fearful that if the truth be told, the relationship will be lost.

One of the ways we grow in love is by overcoming the fear we have about telling the truth. The success of our relationships depends on how honest we permit ourselves to be with ourselves and each other. Love is the freedom to talk about our feelings and the ability to listen when others do the same. When we don't stuff our emotions, we are much less likely to project blame or anger on others. Failure to confront a person about unacceptable behavior is as damaging to a relationship as thoughtless criticism and condemnation. It is especially important for each of us to set a level headed and even tempered atmosphere by approaching the topic with humility instead of an air of superiority or arrogance. The communication can be optimized by the use of "I" statements. For example the formula is "When you_____, I feel _____ because I think _____. This puts the emphasis on our own thoughts and feelings and not on the other person's actions.

When you come home so late at night after so much drinking, I wonder where you've been. Each time I think you might be with another woman, I feel that a great monster is eating me alive bit by bit. I lose another piece of what I value so much and that is the relationship we had five years ago. I remember how much we cared for each other. I miss that feeling of closeness so much, Sometimes I just want to shrivel up and die. And sometimes, I just want to hurt you back. I love you but I see it dying and I don't know what to do about it. I feel helpless, alone and frightened. I often wonder if you feel that way, too.

Love for another is being expressed here through the honest expression of emotional vulnerability and pain. You may be consciously aware that while God may be able to love unconditionally, at this moment you are falling far short of that. You don't have to be a martyr pretending that you don't have angry, resentful, jealous and negative feelings. Sainthood is not required for love; recognition of human limitations is far better.

Jesus repeatedly said, "Verily, verily I say unto you." Or in some translations, "I tell you the truth." And much of what He said and did was radical, shocking and offensive. The "Gospel Truth" was just as offensive to the Pharisees of Jesus' day as it is in many quarters today.

In How People Grow, authors Dr. Henry Cloud and Dr. John Townsend point out that not only was Jesus honest with his disciples, but, in fact, he was committed enough to their spiritual growth to leave them. Jesus told his disciples that sometimes the Heavenly Father will disappear from sight.

I tell you the truth that unless I go away, the Counselor will not come to you. But if I go, I will send him to you.

John 16:7

If that has happened to you, you are likely to think that He is just a fickle friend. But Jesus reassured His followers that there would come a time when everything will be explained. As Oswald Chambers puts it, "Sometimes love has to wait in pain and tears for the blessing of fuller communion." The question we must ask ourselves is: "When God is hidden from us by the clouds of life, do we lose our confidence in Him?"

In his 1978 best seller, The Road Less Traveled, M. Scott Peck, M.D. defined authentic love as, "that which seeks to nurture my own and my loved one's emotional growth." He devotes several chapters to the demands of authentic love. He says that love requires the discipline of being present and attentive, the work of independence and separateness and the risks of commitment, confrontation and loss. He calls it hard work.

The purpose of honesty in relationships is not to "fix others." That is God's job. It is to express who we really are. The message is: "Each of us is valuable and worthy of respect." For example if we tell the truth to ourselves in love, we can give others that courtesy as well. Our motive is not to criticize but to mend fences.

$$\infty$$

Doreen K.: I was not happy about my son's cursing. We have little interaction except by phone. First I had to be honest about the fact that it was disturbing to me. Second, I had to be willing to risk being honest. Third, I had to pray for a non-critical, non-judgmental non-offensive way to tell him how I felt. I said, "When you use curse words and take the Lord's name in vain, it hurts me. The words "Jesus Christ" represent my Lord and Savior. I expect that it's probably just the way you talk with the guys at work and I don't think you mean to deliberately offend me. You know, I think you are smart enough to become bilingual. And I'll bet you could save the tough talk for your buddies and talk to me, your sweet little old English teacher mum in Standard English. Do you think you could handle that?"

$$\infty$$

Tough Love is a form of Paternal Love, the love that corrects. While both Tough Love and Paternal Love have gotten a bad rap, perhaps from authoritarian overtones, maybe we should revisit the concept as an acceptable form of authentic love. Light For My Path is a daily devotional in which I found the following prayer:

> *Sometimes, God, Christians make You sound as though You're a stern joyless taskmaster, waiting to bang us on the head if we so much as color outside the lines. Remind me, Jesus, that this image of the Father is a lie. Thank You that God is a loving parent who always wants the best for me; if You say "no," I know it's only because You want something better for me. Help me to see Your love even in Your correction. Amen*

My son, do not despise the Lord's discipline and do not resent his rebuke, because the Lord disciplines those he loves as a father, the son he delights in.

Proverbs 46:11-12

Gwen S.: I used to think that if I practiced tough love, it would be tough on my kids. I found out that it was excruciatingly tough on me. Tough love meant I had to confront myself and change my ideas and behavior. For so many years I made the mistake of putting the emphasis on the tough, not on the love. It didn't work very well. It didn't give me the results I wanted. It just seemed to set me up for power plays with my teenagers. Their rebellion brought me face to face with my fear of being out of control. I tried to learn from my mistakes. I needed to find a way to stop playing doormat and putting up with unacceptable behavior without surrendering my position of parental authority. My feeling of powerlessness, guilt and shame over my parenting, brought me to my knees and I began to seek God's guidance in prayer. I needed the wisdom and courage to say the right thing at the right time. I had to give up the idea that Tough Love means casting out my loved ones to a hostile universe or that "letting go" means abandoning them to death or chaos. Like so many others who had to learn how to practice tough love, I had to have faith that I was not amputating the relationship but drawing a line in the sand and allowing them to choose their own direction.

∞

Nick H.: It has not been easy to give up hope that one day my relationship with my son would be reciprocal. But now I am satisfied with an occasional phone call letting me know he's OK. He is a unique human being, worthy of dignity, respect and love, no matter what choices he has made in his life. I have finally learned to just love him as he is and let him be who he is. He doesn't need me to be his benefactor, protector, or life skills manager.

∞

Trudy Y.: I had suspected for quite some time that my college-age daughter had a drinking problem. I came home from work one lunch hour, when she was home on vacation, to find her passed out in her bedroom. She was not alone. It was a flagrant violation of house rules. I remembered that "drinking problems" are identified more by what happens when a person drinks than by how much, what, where, when and with whom they drink. I quietly closed the door to her bedroom and went downstairs to gather my thoughts. I went back up stood at the top of the stairs and called to her. "Cindy, I'm home. I am going back out for 15 minutes. When I get home, I expect your guest to be gone and we can talk then." My heart was pounding as I drove around praying for the right words to say. I didn't want to be condemning. I wanted to use this as an opportunity to encourage her to get help.

I was so grateful to find her home when I returned. I was deathly afraid the shame would send her out into the streets. We sat on the couch and I could see her remorse. Since I had also had my own sexual indiscretions it wasn't hard to me to feel great empathy for her. What I said was very simple: "Cindy, I just can't believe you would have deliberately created this situation. You are the only one who knows whether what happened today is a total disregard for our home and disrespect for me as your Mom or a symptom of a drinking problem. You will need to decide whether you want to continue living here or be out on your own. But if you think you need some help with your drinking, it seems that now would be a good time to call a treatment center and schedule an evaluation." She's been clean and sober for more than fifteen years.

∞

Glen F.: There was a time when my oldest son needed me to be strong and it was one of the most difficult things I have ever had to do. He was only thirteen when he got involved in drugs and ran away twice, stealing my car both times. The second time he was gone for five days before I got a call from the police in a distant state telling me they had him in jail. After I brought him home, things went from bad to worse. Valuable articles began to disappear from my house. The thief was one of my son's best friends.

I confronted my young son and told him that there was obviously nothing I could do to deter him from his self-destructive behavior but I was not going to let him destroy my life and my financial security. I gave him a list of ten directives and said that if he was not in full compliance within ten days, he would be choosing to give up living in my home.

That was the most difficult message I had ever had to deliver in my entire life, especially because he was so young. But by allowing his behavior to continue, he would learn that there were no unpleasant consequences for his behavior and I would miss the opportunity to model responsible behavior by standing up for my own rights as a human being.

At the end of the week, I came home from work to find that he and all of his personal belongings were gone. I had no idea where he had gone. I experienced immense fear and pain. I had to believe that someday he would come to understand that, even if he did not value his own life, I valued mine. That was all I had to give him.

> *"I gave him a list of ten directives and said that if he was not in full compliance within ten days, he would be choosing to give up living in my home ."*

Today, twenty five years later, my son and I are close friends. Not long ago he told me, "I love you dad. You never gave up on me." Through this experience I learned that setting consequences was not the same as "giving up" on someone, even though it felt that way at the time. Instead, by exhibiting tough love I was reinforcing to him that even at the tender age of thirteen, he had the ability to make healthy choices.

∞

Families are supposed to support one another in times of trouble. We never want to see our loved ones get hurt. We want to intervene, especially for our children and protect them. But what happens when we have stood in the gap, tried and failed and eventually come to the end of ourselves?

It is very, very difficult to remove ourselves from the buffer zone between their bad decisions or self-destructive behavior and the natural consequences of those actions. It usually takes a long time for us to conclude that we are only postponing the inevitable. They may even be pleading with us not to do them any "favors." It is wise to consider that perhaps the more we enable, in the name of love, the worse the consequences will be, when and if the child, teen or adult, faces up to life on life's terms.

∞

Les and Cheri T.: Our youngest daughter married a semi-functioning alcoholic. We felt very sorry for her in this situation and wanted to make it easier for her and our grandson. After reading Recovery from Rescuing, by Jacqueline Castine, I realized I always focused my time and energy on them while I was being run ragged with the burden of my back breaking generosity. My husband and I knew we needed to make changes. We realized that, while her job was their source of income, her

> *"Even loving and worrying about our daughter and grandson as much as we did, we still had to take that huge risk and let go."*

husband spent recklessly. We firmly stated that we could no longer provide free child care and that unless she could pay me she would have to find it elsewhere. We also told our daughter that her husband was welcome in our home but his beer was not. Even loving and worrying about our daughter and grandson as much as we did, we still had to take that huge risk and let go. I don't have to tell you that emotions were running mighty high!! But the gamble paid off. She finally asked her husband to leave. I can not tell you the change in my daughter since. She is only 22 but has worked herself up to a respectable position in the Accounting Department of a large newspaper. She and our other daughter bought a townhouse together and are living independently. We lent, not gave, them the down payment and they pay us back monthly. Our grandson has been home with me during the daytime. Next week he starts preschool and I'm off to Yoga!!! Life is good!

∞

My Mom's Alzheimer's is progressing. She is ninety-one and has been fiercely independent since my father died over twenty-five years ago. Frequently, I am put in a position where I must ask myself when to take charge and when to let go. We were raised with a controlling hand and didn't question her authority. Now I am faced with her anger when I attempt to "supervise" the medication or the finances. There have been some lapses, with serious fallouts, which I would like to prevent in the future. Of course with this brain disorder, there is no "learning from consequences," thus no opportunity to self-correct. Insight and judgment will continue to fade. I know that it is just a question of time before her prized independence will be diminished, one freedom at a time. Control of finances will be followed by relinquishing the car keys. Ultimately there will be a change in her living situation. I expect a struggle with tears on both sides. We love her; we are proud that she has been so healthy and independent for such a long time. She is an amazing example of graceful aging to everyone who knows her. We are grateful that she is not in physical pain. My sister and I grow even closer as we support each other and grieve the gradual loss of our Mother to this awful disease. And we are confident that our Higher Power will see all three of us through this difficult business of tough love living and dying.

∞

In both Hebrew and Greek, love is translated as an action indicating conscious acts on behalf of a beloved. However Biblical love seems to demand going beyond a particular behavior to include a certain inner attitude, that is, a positive inner response. Paul calls love the greatest gift of all.

> *If I speak in the tongues of men and of angels, but have not love, I am only a resounding gong or a clanging cymbal. If I have the gift of all prophecy and can fathom all mysteries and all knowledge, and if I have a faith that can move mountains but have not love, I am nothing. If I give all I possess to the poor and surrender my body to the flames, but have not love, I gain nothing.*

> *Love is patient, love is kind, it does not envy, it does not boast, it is not proud. It is not rude, it is not self-seeking, it is not easily angered, it keeps no record of wrongs. Love does not delight in evil but rejoices with the truth. It always protects, always trusts, always hopes, always perseveres.*

I Corinthians 13:1-8

The Bible tells us that without God's power we are incapable of love that is unselfish. No amount of wishing for it, or striving for it, will make it so.

My friend in Texas called the other day to talk about her husband's progressing Alzheimer's disease. He is a minister. She had been invited to attend a women's retreat and wanted very much to attend. She has two daughters who could easily have taken over but her husband would have had to go to their homes this would have been quite a change in his schedule. She said, "You know, in the end, as much as I was looking forward to it, I just couldn't leave him in the care of the girls because no matter what we did, he would know why we did it. And it would be acknowledging that he is no longer a responsible person. There will come a time for that, somewhere down the line, but I want to avoid it as long as I can." She says living with this disease requires patience, as we all know. But she really hit home with me when she said, "It is hard not to say 'I told you that three times already'."

∞

Perhaps you have heard the expression, "Forgiveness is the fragrance of the flower that clings to the shoe that crushed it." Though we have not been able to locate the source of this wisdom, there is a scene from Les Misérables, the 1998 film based on Victor Hugo's novel, that exemplifies this extraordinary form of mercy and love.

> *"Forgiveness is the fragrance of the flower that clings to the shoe that crushed it."*

In the opening scene we see Liam Neeson as Jean Valjean. He has just been released on parole from prison in 18th century France. He had served nineteen years at hard labor for stealing bread to feed his family and is now wandering the countryside hungry and homeless. He is told to knock at the door of the local abbey to ask for food. Though it is well past dark, the Bishop answers the knocking and the hooded Valjean asks,

"Do you have any food you can spare for me?"

"Come in," the Bishop replies.

"I'm a convict. I'm out on parole. Here are my papers."

"I know who you are. You're welcome to come in and eat with us."

"You mean you are going to let me in?"

At dinner the housekeeper asks, "What crime did you commit?"

Valjean replies, "Maybe I killed someone. How do you know I am not a murderer?"

"How do you know that I'm not a murderer?" retorts the clergyman.

"Well, I'm not a murderer, I'm a thief. I stole food and I paid for my crime by spending nineteen years in chains at hard labor."

"Men can be unjust, but not God."

During the night Valjean is awakened by a nightmare. He gets dressed, goes into the kitchen and, as he is in the process of putting all of the hostelry silver utensils in his knapsack, he is discovered by his host. When the Bishop confronts him, Valjean knocks him down and flees.

The following morning the Bishop is tending his garden and the housekeeper is complaining that now they will be eating with wooden utensils. Just as he tells her that he wants no more discussion about the incident, the local police burst onto the scene with Valjean in handcuffs. The constable announces "We found this man up the road."

"Didn't he tell you he was our guest?"

"Yes, after we searched his belonging and found the silver. He claimed you gave it to him."

"Well, yes, of course. But Jean, I'm angry with you. Why didn't you take the candlesticks too? They are worth at least 2000 francs. Now, here, take them, and be on your way. He has to get going. He has lost a lot of time."

As the constable releases Valjean from his handcuffs, the Bishop takes him by the shoulders, looks him straight in the eye and says, "And don't forget . . . don't ever forget you promised, my brother, that you, Jean Valjean, would become a new man. You no longer belong to evil. I bought you back with this silver—a ransom for fear and hatred. And now I give you back to God.

∞

No chapter on the subject of love would complete without a discussion about loving ourselves. People who are continually focused on meeting the needs of other people often need

> *"God wants a living sacrifice, not a dead one."*

a brush up on self-love and self-nurturing. It is easy to forget that there is a middle ground between selfish and selfless. We, who wish to be sensitive to others, need also to be aware of our own wants and needs.

I like the expression: "God wants a living sacrifice, not a dead one." It was joyful news to me because I knew that I was one of those people who simply was not willing to sacrifice myself, or my life, to care for my mentally ill, abusive children. And I am not alone.

∞

Mary Lou E.: I am the mother of four. One of them had a serious mental illness for many years. I found it necessary to withdraw out of self-protection. I just couldn't be a participant in her illness with all the paranoia and manipulative games. When I withdrew out of self-protection, she thought it was lack of love and accused me of being disloyal. She turned on me with hate and venomous diatribes. Later she told me her psychiatrist said I had done the right thing. It's never easy to disengage. Every now and then I am overwhelmed by the awareness that I lost one of my four children. You know, I think I really had no choice. I think the choice was made for me by my character. I could have been either an enabler or withdraw: A or B. And because of my particular nature, which I think I had little control over, I chose to save myself. I simply couldn't deal with the "mess."

∞

Sarah Ban Breathnach, who wrote <u>Simple Abundance, a Daybook of Comfort and Joy;</u> says she lives by the philosophy, "Do unto myself as I know God wants me to do unto others." I have found that support, solitude, sobriety and spiritual connection are the tools that serve me well in the self-nurturing department of my life.

Patricia H. Livingston, author of <u>This Blessed Mess</u>, describes a time in her life when she was reeling from a divorce and went to a trusted Jesuit priest. He told her he was going to send her on a mission. Thinking that she would need to sell her possessions, get shots, and learn a foreign language, she soon learned he had other ideas. He told her that of all the missions God entrusts us with at birth, among the most important is to "Go to yourself." He instructed her to go to the cosmetic specialty shop, buy a fine bar of soap, a lovely hand towel with embroidery and lace and some fragrant lotion. "Wash your hands tenderly several times each day for the next month," he said, "and each time you do it let yourself feel how much God loves you." Pat Livingston writes that it is important for us to understand that, "Love your neighbor as yourself" means that in order to give freely to others without losing our self worth, we need to attend to ourselves with real reverence. The Priest told her, "When you die God will not ask you, "What did you accomplish?" or "How perfect did you become?" but rather, "How did you care for My friend?"

> *"It is important for us to understand that 'Love your neighbor as yourself' means that in order to give freely to others without losing our self- worth, we need to attend to ourselves with real reverence."*

∞

Part of self-love is the ability to ask for what we need and to receive it. Ask God to reveal His purpose for your life. What activities give you joy? If you can't think of anything that gives you pleasure, it is most certainly time to try some new experiences. Spend time alone. Develop the gentle art of cocooning. Regenerate from within. Or do something to shake yourself out of your pattern. Take tap-dancing lessons. Join a support group. Do more of what's easy and fun. Where are your natural talents?

∞

In January of 1987, my two daughters seemed stabilized from their turbulent adolescences. I peeked out from behind the wall of demands and responsibilities which had boxed me into a traditional life. It looked like the coast was clear and I made my break. I resigned my corporate sales position and took myself on a 15,000-mile road trip across the sun belt of the United States. I called it "Time Out for Good Behavior." It was not an escape, but rather a celebration—a reward—a revival—a re-creation. I combined miles of beautiful, scenic, driving time alone with visiting my network of friends who were strung out across the country. In my willingness to experience uncertainty and loneliness, I found that I was never lonely. The experience was a meditation.

Most, but not all, of my friends and family were overjoyed for me. Some questioned my sanity; some were angry, others jealous. My daughters who were both in college said, "Mother, we think you could have found a more convenient time to have your mid-life crisis." I knew that if I waited for permission, I would never do it.

What else did I gain? I found out some of the things I love to do when I'm not doing for everyone else. I found out that I am as good a friend to myself as I have been to others. I am good company and trustworthy. I, who had overcome a phobia of driving on freeways in my twenties, gained a new respect for myself.

Often those who love, live and work with individuals who have addictions and mental illness say they have focused so much on the needs of others for so long that they do not have any idea what they want to do, or even like to do. What about you? You don't have to leave home to have a discovery adventure. Ask yourself:

1. How do I like to play when I'm not playing the role of parent, employee, child, sibling or spouse?

2. What do I like to do when I don't <u>have</u> to do anything?

3. What do I have when I have only me?

4. Why am I here on earth? What is my purpose in living?

The following are some awareness exercises:

These are five things I love to touch:

_____
_____
_____
_____
_____

These are five things I love to see:

_____
_____
_____
_____
_____

These are five things I love to hear:

_____
_____
_____
_____
_____

These are five things I love to smell:

_____
_____
_____

_____

_____

These are five unforgettable moments in my life:

_____

_____

_____

_____

_____

These are five activities that I enjoy:

_____

_____

_____

_____

_____

These are five relationships I most treasure:

_____

_____

_____

_____

_____

These are five things I want to do in the next 10 years:

_____

_____

_____

_____

_____

HELPING

...what works, what doesn't and why...

Help, v.- *To contribute strength or means to, render assistance to, cooperate effectively with, to relieve someone in need, pain, sickness, distress. A means of remedying or stopping something. Furnishing anything that furthers another's efforts or relieves his wants or necessities.*
                    Random House Dictionary of the English Language

Rescue, v.- *To free or deliver from confinement, violence, danger or evil. Syn. liberate, release, save, redeem, ransom, extricate.*
                    Random House Dictionary of the English Language

Fix, v.- *repair, mend, restore, doctor, fix up, patch, patch up, touch up, renovate, renew, correct, amend, rectify, remedy, better, ameliorate, adjust, arrange, stabilize, straighten, place, clasp, castrate.*
                    The Synonym Finder, Jerome. I. Rodale

Control, v.- *dominate, rule over, reign over, govern, command, order, dictate, have it all one's own way, call the shots, call the plays, run the show, boss, lay down the law, hold the purse strings, be in the driver's seat, be in the saddle, wear the pants, be in a position of authority, hold all the cards, have well in hand, be master of the situation, be on top of, have under one's thumb, intimidate, suppress, restrain, hold back, ride herd on, gain the upper hand, regulate, rule the roost, wear the crown, tyrannize, hold captive.*
                    The Synonym Finder, Jerome I. Rodale

Please put your own oxygen mask in place before assisting your children.
          Airlines flight attendant's preflight safety directions to passengers.

HELPING

.

Why, you may ask, is there a discussion of "helping," in a book targeted for people who have already done everything they could think of to help, without results? The questions we ask ourselves here are: "In any given situation or relationship, does the helping help?" "Who does it help?" "If helping, fixing, controlling doesn't help, then what do we do?" The personal stories on this topic reflect how some people moved forward in their own lives, and their relationships, when they gave up trying to help. There are some practical and spiritual principles in these stories that work in special circumstances. Take what seems best for you and leave the rest.

When I was about seven years old, I remember having a strong FIXation! Walking home from school every day, I observed the middle class Detroit neighborhood where we lived. I often had thoughts and dreams about one day having some kind of supernatural ability to fix it up. I was acutely aware of how much was broken, unsightly, dirty, cluttered and disorderly. My desire was to repair everything that was fragmented, tear down what was unsightly, haul away the trash in the alleys, create order out of chaos, whitewash what was sooty, declutter the yards, make everything shiny, bright and new. I wanted to make my environment to be beautiful, orderly, perfect. I guess I was in the "diagnose and treat" business, even at such a tender age. In other words I wanted the world to "shape up!"

As I think back on this, I wonder where this disposition came from. Was it a passion to make the world a better place? Was it a projection of the internal chaos I felt as a child living in an alcoholic family? Did I have a burning desire to control something outside of myself, because I had so little control at home. No wonder then, that I have such a compulsion to be in charge!

As a mover, shaker, fixer-upper, doer, activist, and hyper-activist, I find it challenging to see that Scripture assures me that I can never get to heaven through good works and that there is no evidence in the Bible that "God helps those who help themselves." And my own spiritual experience reinforces that I am basically useless to God without my faith in Him. I am reminded of that every time I start to operate under my own steam. And of course, I saw just how much God could do for me when I lost the thing I was most prideful about . . . my mind. . . when I could do nothing to help myself.

∞

Dolores Howell: After exams, in May of 1970, our oldest son, Tom, returned home from Michigan State in Lansing where he had been studying for a competitive scholarship. He was in a state of catatonia. We had no idea why he just stared into space and couldn't answer simple questions or resume the family pattern.

"After one of his suicide attempts, we had a family meeting, where everyone offered something they could do to help him."

We took him to our pediatrician, who said Tom was very depressed. In fact, he was suicidal. We saw a psychiatrist and, by nightfall, our son was hospitalized in a psychiatric facility. He was medicated, but we were not given a diagnosis. Things seemed to return to normal for awhile. Then a few years later, our son was diagnosed as bipolar. Lithium was prescribed to stabilize his mood. It worked. The hospital social worker seemed convinced that we, the parents, were the cause of Tom's illness. "People shouldn't have more children than arms," she said. I guess we were three over quota. I discounted the "mother did it" theory and dealt with the situation the best I could.

We are a family of faith and our prayers always included Tom. We prayed to be able to say the right things to the right people at the right time and to somehow relieve his suffering. We certainly knew we couldn't do it alone.

As the years passed, Tom seemed to stabilize. But following a divorce, he was again hospitalized. This time he reported that voices were controlling him. Psychotropic drugs were added to the lithium and he was religious about taking his medication. He once asked for an exorcism to rid himself of these demons that plagued him constantly. Once his depression was so severe, he was given six electroconvulsive therapy treatments (ECT) or "Shock Therapy."

All of us in the family had our own struggles with his illness. His brothers and sister tried to understand him and include him in their activities. By this time, he lost most of his friends because he could become belligerent. After one of his suicide attempts, we had a family meeting, where everyone offered something they could do to help him. One son said he would find something to compliment every time he saw him, to lift his self esteem. Another son said he could help with his car repairs. Others said they would include him in their activities when possible. One son said he could live with him, so he wouldn't be lonely. We were a family to be proud of that day.

In 1985, I found the Alliance for the Mentally Ill (AMI). This organization was a beacon of hope. They gave us the latest information on brain disorders and I became active in both local and national Alliance affairs. I attended almost every state and national convention around the country and served more than two years as the local chapter president. I felt I could really help the stigma situation by talking about mental illness everywhere: in churches, meetings, with friends. My son shared this interest and went with me, frequently speaking from the patient's perspective. He began working with others who were in recovery from mental illness.

Sadly in 2001, our son died suddenly from a dissected ascending aorta after emergency surgery. The church was filled with his family and friends who spoke in tribute to how much he had touched their lives. He organized Friday night card games, took friends out to play pool, concerts, picnics, parks, etc. at his expense. Sometimes he would just visit those who had no friends. He was only 47, but his life was a testimony to how much good can come from so much chaos. As our family tried to envelop him with love and support, we became more cohesive. His life helped all of us survive other traumas as a unit.

∞

I was privileged to work with Dolores on the Board of Directors of the South Oakland Citizens for the Homeless (SOCH). She wrote this tribute for her son and to let people know about the benefits of becoming involved in a chapter of the Alliance for the Mentally Ill. Dolores died suddenly from the same condition that took her son, just a few weeks after she submitted her story. We all miss her.

The story of the Howell family is an inspiring example of how support can be a give and take healing factor for individuals, families, groups and organizations. And it reminds us that givers become receivers and receivers become givers through this process.

∞

Frank and Priscilla: My wife and I began our experience with the bipolar disorder in 1988. It began with an alarming phone call from our son. He was experiencing hallucinations and delusions. We were completely ignorant about what was going on. Fifteen years and sixteen hospitalizations later, it is still a worry.

We have tried everything to help him: family therapy, punishment, pep talks, the best doctors and counselors. We encouraged him. Nothing seemed to help. He would go along for a few months, even two years without any major episodes. But as soon as we thought he had turned the corner and had control over the symptoms, he would relapse. What made matters worse was his addiction to alcohol and his dependence on marijuana.

Looking back, I can see that he never respected the illness. He never took the steps to understand the illness and, as a result of his lack of knowledge, he could not take effective care of himself. For example he would not curtail the pot, alcohol, cigarettes or heavy caffeine. His eating habits were poor; he did not take the prescribed medications and then could not keep any kind of a regular sleeping pattern. He seemed to lack the insight to do what was best for himself. No matter what anyone in the family said or did for him, he perceived it as our trying to take control of him. We perceived it as trying to help him control the illness so he could control his life. And now we see that our trying to help him interfered with him obtaining the feedback he needed to gain the insight to help himself.

> *"No matter what anyone in the family said, or did for him, he perceived it as our trying to take control of him. We perceived it as trying to help him control the illness so he could control his life."*

∞

We conclude that fixing, helping and supporting is valuable if it works. If you feel good giving assistance and those receiving it find your assistance beneficial, there is not a problem.

On the other hand, if 1) trying to fix relationships or people you perceive as "broken" has been making you crazy 2) you are not getting the results you hope for 3) others don't appreciate what you do for them and they are rejecting you or 4) you wish the other person would take more responsibility for their own well-being, then perhaps you should look at your own behavior pattern and stop focusing on theirs. Maybe we don't know how to separate ourselves from our children's problems without divorcing ourselves from them. Maybe we notice that just as we get rid of one dependency problem, another crops up before we have a chance to catch our breath. Here are some questions that you might consider as you decipher what is helping and what is enabling in your relationships. It's helpful to ask,

"How does my rescuing or helping behavior make me feel? How does it make the other person feel? What result am I getting? Do I want a change in their behavior, attitude or lifestyle? How about my own?"

It takes two to play the rescuing game: the helper and the helped, the alcoholic and the enabler, the dependent and the codependent, the doctor and the patient, the shoulder to lean on and the heavy depressed head. Maybe you are just getting tired, and growing resentful. Maybe after a lifetime of service to others you wonder if the burden of caring for others is making you sick. You may have found you've invited a bear to dance (or accepted an invitation from the bear) and now you can't sit down until the bear gets tired. What started out as fun has become exhausting. Maybe you're beginning to wish that someone might come along to rescue you!

∞

In her best seller, <u>The Dance of Anger</u>, Harriet Lerner, Ph.D. describes a classic scenario between siblings. The "responsible" sister is very disgusted with the behavior of her chronically in-crisis younger brother. The chapter is called "My Brother is a Mess!" She is angry because he borrows money, doesn't pay it back, asks for her advice and doesn't follow it. Then she feels guilty about sounding unsympathetic and complaining. She is really worried about him. The author describes this merry-go-round between the helper and the helped as a circular dance; both are locked into their own synchronized step patterns. As psychologist Dr. Lerner notes, the more the sister over-functions, the more her brother under-functions. The less the "helper" fails to show any vulnerability by expressing her doubts, frustration and feelings of powerlessness to the "helpee," the more helpless he becomes. The author points out that those relationships become very polarized when one person is expressing only weakness and the other only competence.

∞

The *Dear Abby* column often deals with the frustrations of people who write to her regarding family relationships related to mental illness and addiction. Many describe the guilt, fear and uncertainty of coping with their own feelings while simultaneously trying to help their relatives.

One woman wrote to say she was concerned about her sister's relationship with a depressed woman at church who was going through a divorce and was "very needy." She said her sibling used to have a lot of good friends but now that this one person has taken over her life, Sis is stressed to the point of burnout. Abby replied, "This sounds like a one sided relationship in which your sister, probably in a desire to rescue someone in pain, has become so involved in another's well-being that she has forgotten her own needs. This isn't a healthy situation for your sister or this unfortunate woman, who may be in need of professional counseling. Listening and empathizing with another person's problems is part of friendship but giving and solicitousness, taken to extremes, can have a definite downside."

It isn't just adults who can be burdened with trying to save a loved one from addiction. A 13-year-old wrote *Dear Abby* to say that she was court ordered to live with her dad because her mom was on drugs and "doing bad things to get money." She wrote, "It was better living with Dad but we missed Mom. The judge said mom could have us overnight if she got into a program. She isn't in the program anymore and she blames us for not visiting her. I always cry after she calls. I'm afraid she'll take a drug overdose and die. Dad told me Mom is sick. I want to forget my mom but I can't. What can I do to stop crying every night?"

The columnist advised the young lady to talk to her dad. She said "From your description your mother does appear to be ill and out of touch with reality. When people have heartaches like yours, the surest way to resolve is to share them. You cannot 'save your mom;' only she can do that. And for your own sake, you must not allow her to make you feel guilty. Sometimes when a situation is out of control it has to be left to a higher power. Keep busy and if the crying continues I urge you to ask your dad to help you get professional counseling."

When counseling a young mother whose husband accuses her of "over reacting to his drinking," Abby recommends locating a chapter of Al-Anon (888) 425-2666 or going to the website www.al-anon.alateen.org. She states, "Your husband's behavior won't change until he realizes he has a problem and wants to do something about it. Whether you want to spend the rest of your life this way is a question only you can answer. But please realize that a tendency toward alcoholism can be inherited, and be sure your children understand that fact as they grow older."

∞

I believe most women would agree that our hot buttons for helping were installed genetically and nurtured socially, if not scripturally. I want to be (and to be thought of as) a good person, a loving mother, a kind neighbor, a contributing member of the community. I want approval. I don't want anyone to accuse me of not doing my duty. I am afraid of criticism. I am afraid that if I don't do it, no one else will pick up the slack. I get anxious if I'm not making a contribution. I like the feeling of being needed. Actually, I get a rush of adrenalin when someone asks me for help.

Because I uncovered my "fix-it fixation" in the context of learning about chemical dependency, I like to talk about my own enabling as an addiction. We addicts always feel guilty if we say "NO." "YES" is mandatory, not a choice! If you don't have a predisposition to addictive behavior, you can probably enjoy helping others on a selective basis, free to choose when it is convenient for you to do so. You don't have an attraction to it. You can control it. It doesn't control your life. Like a glass of wine before dinner or a casual beer at the ball game, helping someone just gives you a nice warm relaxed feeling about other people and life. You won't be uncomfortable if you abstain.

An enabler is a compulsive helper, someone who cannot keep from stepping in to give aid, even when it is unsolicited. I found that my behavior was the outer projection of my inner belief that there is a right way to live, a right way to do things. It was my way, of course. Thus it was my duty, obligation and responsibility to get everyone on the right path and keep them there at all costs. I was in the "diagnose and treat business," whether in the role of wife, mother, teacher or consultant.

Like substance abuse, compulsive work or gambling, enabling helps people avoid their own underlying relationship issues. If you suspect that your helping behavior is keeping a loved one helpless, or if you are uncomfortable and resentful because others don't take your advice or appreciate your efforts to help, you may be moving from constructive helping to addictive enabling.

Enabling supports negative behavior by protecting a person from the consequences of their behavior. If you try to keep the "problem" safely tucked away or "cover" the troubles, you contribute to the problem. In addition to depriving an individual of the opportunities to grow and learn through mistakes, the message you communicate is that they are incapable of growing up and becoming responsible. If you let them dump all of their problems on your ears only, you prevent them from getting the professional help they often need. If you are writing excuses, paying the bills, making the phone calls and absorbing the anxiety of the problem, the other person is off the hook. She or he has someone else doing all the work. And she or he may not be the only one with a "problem!"

Author Harriet Lerner, in The Dance of Anger, says some of us want the impossible. We want to control not only our own decisions and choices but also the other person's reactions to them. We not only want to make a change; we want the other person to like the change that we make. We want to move ahead to a higher level of assertiveness and clarity and then receive praise and reinforcement from those very people who have chosen us for our old familiar ways.

I used to believe that if I didn't do it, no one else would. There was a time when my low self-esteem was always striving to raise itself to a morally superior position. Helping was one of those ladders. Now I ask myself, "Can I create intimacy only with those who need me? Does my attention to others keep the focus off my own needs? Do I think I shouldn't have any needs?"

In addition, I am very likely to fall back into my addiction to helping by my perception, or misperception, of "their need." Maybe this is one of your stumbling blocks, too. Often adult relationships, based solely on needs are destructive in some way. When I am presented with a situation which appears to require my assistance, or a request for help, the first thing I want to investigate is my motive for helping. I've learned that I'm vulnerable to manipulation by others when I am not honest with myself. So I ask myself: "Do I have an agenda? Whose interest will I be serving? Am I expecting a 'pay off?' Is it love? Approval? Gratitude? Do I want a change in the other person or the situation? Am I afraid to say no? What are my needs in this situation? Do I want to do this? How will I feel if I do? If I don't?" I try to remember that there can be a balance in my relationships. There is middle ground between dancing while joined at the hip and casting the offending member out of my circle altogether.

∞

Since fixing can be both helpful and destructive, here are some questions you might ask yourself if you wonder what motivates your behavior.

THE RESCUER'S QUIZ

1. Has the primary focus in your life been toward serving the needs of others?

2. Are you in, or drawn to, one of the service professions: teaching, nursing, social work, the ministry?

3. Have there been addicted people in your family? Father? Mother? Siblings?

4. Has your self-esteem been wrapped around your image of yourself as a super-mom or super-neighbor or the guy who's the last to leave the office at night?

5. Are you the first one through the door with a casserole when somebody dies?

6. Are you the oldest child in the family? Are you the one everyone depends on to do the job, and to do it right?

7. When you attend a lecture or a class, do you always think, "Oh, Mary should be here. She would really benefit from this." As you are reading this book, are you thinking about who else *needs* to read it?

8. Is it hard for you to take time for yourself and have fun?

9. Do you believe you are responsible for making other people happy?

10. Do you find yourself being resented when you were only trying to help?

11. Do you find yourself giving advice that is not welcome or accepted?

12. Do you think you know what is best for other people?

13. Do you often feel that no matter how much you do, it isn't enough?

14. Has the pleasure you used to get from loving and caring given way to feelings of exhaustion and resentment

15. Are you especially critical of others who don't do their share?

16. Are you feeling somewhat defensive about any of your answers? For example, the thought may have crossed your mind, "Of course, I can't relax and have any fun. My whole life has been tied up with taking care of mother since my sister and her husband retired to play golf in Florida."

There aren't any right or wrong answers to this quiz. It's just a tool to help you assess your pattern and vulnerabilities. But if you would like to change your situation, it is always helpful to stop making excuses for it.

∞

Melanie M.: I have always wanted to fix everything for everyone, keep peace in all relationships and protect people—-even in those relationships where I'm not involved. I have recently found myself stretching the truth and omitting facts to keep the peace between daughter and husband, brother and father.

My daughter does not handle things well when they don't go her way—although maturity is helping in that area. She feels that I, as her mother, should be doing certain things to make her happy. So to enjoy her company I am constantly doing for her, even when I really don't have time to do it, whatever it is.

Last summer, I realized that I no longer could spend the energy being SO VERY careful of her needs and that she could, in fact, take care of them herself. And that I needed to take care of myself. Now when I hear the question at home or at a meeting, "Will you take care of this?" I try to stay silent for a few moments and think to myself, "Do I have time, energy or desire to say yes or can someone else do it?" I also think, "What will I get from this? Will this help me in my life?" It's the most difficult moment for me and it takes practiced discipline. I am no longer jumping when someone else wants me to jump! It's not that I don't care about others feelings; it's just that I have to protect my life and newly found peace and serenity.

The benefits have been outstanding. I have gained some confidence in my ability to take care of myself. I have less of other people's business to take care of. People at church are amazed that I am letting go and not signing up for next year's projects. My daughter has more self-esteem, knowing that she's taking care of things she should be taking care of. I have more time to take care of me.

∞

For those readers who have not yet run out of options, here are some ways to help, not enable, people with addictions and mental illness while still maintaining appropriate boundaries.

I. THE COACHING APPROACH: (An Example)

The June 20[th.] 2004 issue of <u>Parade Magazine,</u> ran a cover story ("Too Tough to Seek Help?") about professional football player Terry Bradshaw's struggle with clinical depression. Authors Dianne Hales and Dr. Robert Hales outlined the following practical advice:

- Express your concern, but don't nag. You might say, "I'm concerned about you. You are struggling right now. We need to find some help."
- Don't be distracted by behaviors like drinking or gambling, which often disguise male depression.
- Don't accept resistance at face value. If a man says, "I don't need help," or "It won't do any good," make the appointment yourself and go with him if necessary.
- Provide emotional support. "Your tough guy may need some comforting, some drawing out," says Surgeon Richard Carmona. "Don't let him withdraw or sulk. Listen carefully. Gently insist that he come with you on walks or outings."
- Do not ignore remarks about suicide. Report them to his doctor or, in an emergency, call 911.
- Encourage him to remain in treatment until symptoms begin to subside (which can take several weeks.)

II. THE CONTRACT APPROACH (An Example)

September 16, 2002

Lance, here are your options:

We all want to help you. The problem has been that you only want part of the help—like money for cigarettes, rent, food, and gas. You have turned down the mental health part of the help. This problem has been repeating for years. You can stop this vicious cycle now, with the right kind of professional help and our strong support. We love you very much. Starting today, the only way we will support your physical needs is for you to agree to the following:

- Stay away from alcohol and drugs.
- Get back on the Lithium.

- Agree to full evaluation and follow their recommendation, if you are suicidal.
- Follow through with short-term hospitalization and community mental health case management, if recommended.
- Become stable so you can apply for that job you really want.
- Continue with therapy while you have your job.

This will give you a fresh new start and we will continue to give you all the moral support you need.

Love, Dad & Mom

III. THE "CODE BLUE" APPROACH (An Example)

Sometimes a decision to stop trying to fix things, gives us the freedom and energy to experience more compassion and understanding. A friend of mine who works as a floor nurse in an ICU spoke to me of the "Code Blue" phenomenon she has observed in her duties. She relates that sometimes, after everything medically possible has been done to aid a dying patient, all support systems are withdrawn and a blue sign is hung over the bed. When the medical attention stops, the patient mysteriously and spontaneously improves. Can you think of what ways you might apply the "Code Blue" Approach to your own relationships?

To underscore the benefits of benign neglect, Steve Sternberg of USA Today reported some research findings of the American Heart Association in February, 2004. The study revealed that women who were closely embraced by family and friends after a heart attack are three times more likely to have another attack—possibly a fatal one. The implication is that pitching in to help a woman with life threatening heart disease may not be the best thing for her. Having lots of loving and concerned people around may add to her stress and trigger the habit that she must look after those all those worried people who are in her own house. Men who get support don't seem to have any of these responses or feel the need to reciprocate, the article stated.

∞

In my own family, the whole time I was trying to get my children off drugs and alcohol, not much happened. When I gave up, they got into treatment on their own accord, because they could see that I was not the one making their lives unmanageable. I continued to tell them that I loved and cared about them, even in the face of chronic mental illness or addictions.

I know I am helping out of love when I have the freedom to let go of expectations and outcomes. I know I am helping out of love when I avoid giving unsolicited advice. I know I am helping out of love when I communicate "I" messages respectfully in a low keyed way. For example, I might say "It sounds like your life isn't going very well right now. I'm so sorry to hear that." Or "I wish I could fix it all up but to tell the truth, I've got a lot of stress in my life right now too. I want you to know I worry about you when I don't hear from you and then I get anxious when you do call because I really don't have the answers for your life." This kind of response balances enmeshment with empathy. It is important to convey support while maintaining healthy separateness.

Helping seems most effective when it encourages the other person to help himself or herself. I always hope I can empower a person in trouble to see themselves with new eyes and to focus on their potential. I always hope to encourage them to make decisions about their own situation.

∞

The following is borrowed from the literature of Families Anonymous, a self-help support group (see Appendix) and summarizes most of the more important concepts that have been presented in this chapter.

HELPING

My role as helper is not to do things for the person I am trying to help, but to be things; not to try to control and change his actions, but through understanding and awareness, to change my reactions. I will change my negatives to positives, fear to faith, contempt for what he does to respect for the potential within him, hostility to understanding and manipulation or over-protectiveness to release with love: not trying to make him fit a standard or image, but giving him an opportunity to pursue his own destiny, regardless of what his choice may be. I will change my dominance to encouragement, panic to serenity, the inertia of despair to the energy of my own personal growth and self-justification to self-understanding.

Self-pity blocks effective action. The more I indulge in it, the more I feel that the answer to my problems is a change in others and in society, not in myself. Thus I become a hopeless case.

Exhaustion is the result when I use my energy in mulling over the past with regret, or in trying to figure ways to escape a future that has yet to arrive. Projecting an image of the future and anxiously hovering over it for fear that it will or it won't come true, uses all my energy and leaves me unable to live today. Yet living today is the only way to have a life.

I will have no thought for the future actions of others, neither expecting them to be better nor worse as time goes on, for in such expectations I am really trying to create. I will love and let be.

All people are always changing. If I try to judge them, I do so only on what I think I know of them, failing to realize that there is much I do not know. I will give others credit for attempts at progress and for having had many victories which are unknown.

I, too, am always changing, and I can make that change a constructive one, if I am willing. I can change myself. Others I can only love.

∞

SOMEWHERE IN THE SHADOWS

Glancing over Your shoulder
Peering 'round the corner,
I sensed you were there today.
I had set my eyes on my desire
and taken a few tottering steps forward.
But out of the corner of my eye
I caught you smiling
And I tumbled,
Suddenly self-conscious.
But you didn't rush to scoop me into Your arms
or kiss my scraped knees.
You pretended not to see
so I would forget that I had fallen.
And in some strange
and paradoxical way
I loved you more in that gift
of self-chosen absence
than in Your presence.

From <u>Emergence: Poems from the Journey</u> © 1999
by Elaine Jarvis

∞

<u>Linda B</u>.: *Whenever you are tempted to "caretake," imagine a big beautiful silver airplane at the far end of the runway. Say to your child, spouse, or significant other, silently, "You were meant to fly. Let me get off the runway. Beautiful journey. Safe return."*

LISTENING

...hearing with new ears...

When we suspend our need for agreement,
When we are willing to listen for understanding,
When we are truly attentive,
When we are not just biding time to present our side,
We reap great rewards in communication.

James Tongue

Listening is loving.

Jackie Castine

Listen, v. - *harken, hark, pay attention, give heed, prick up one's ears, give an ear to, be attentive to, give one's full attention, be all ears, hang on every word.*

The Synonym Finder, Jerome. I. Rodale

All kinds of animals, birds, reptiles and creatures of the sea are being tamed and have been tamed by man, but no man can tame the tongue. It is a restless evil, full of deadly poison.

James 3:7

LISTENING

<u>Patti M</u>.: If I am not a danger to myself or anyone else, why do I feel like a basket case after a conversation with my Mother? I wonder if she even knows what she does to my state of mind during our little Monday night chats wherein she throws casual comments about serious things around like beanbags. Does she expect me to ignore them as a cause for worry and possible action? How could she not know that they always prey heavily upon my responsible, first-born mind? Why, when I try to treat her like a friend and share my confidences, does she try to analyze them, assess blame, and come up with fixes for them? There are no fixes asked for, or required. It does seem to be a trait that runs in the family. Excuse me for being human, but sometimes a friend just emotes to another friend without anything required, except a patient listening ear. I guess that being a mother makes it different.

∞

Who has been most helpful to you in sorting out your own real life dramas? Chances are you would say this person is a good listener. It is probably not your mother. Mothers get hooked into our stuff. And vice-versa. They installed our hot buttons, as the saying goes. They are emotionally involved and rightfully so. They are entrenched stakeholders in our problems and our well-being. But then perhaps your mother is the problem person you can't fix.

Therapists, ministers and trusted friends are often our best source when we need to talk about what frustrates us. They listen; some are professionally trained to listen. They give us the feeling that they are on our side, and that they are our allies because they understand our dilemma. They stand with us as we work on sifting and sorting through our 'stuff'. We may also notice that these people function as a "sounding board." This useful role reflects back to us what we say and how we feel without the distortion of fault-finding judgment—-of another person, a situation or us. This interested, yet relatively neutral, observer trusts that we have the capacity to figure things out for ourselves. We come away from the exchange with a greater sense of clarity, understanding and empowerment.

∞

Lauren N.: The phone rang at 6:45 AM and my daughter Sarah asked, "Is this too early?" It was, but I listened. And I listened. I did not give an opinion. I did not comment. I did not give advice. But I must confess that during her monologue, I was multi-tasking: listening to her and talking to myself. A little voice inside me said, "Isn't this nice? You aren't asking probing questions about her sibling, forcing her to 'report' to you. You aren't upset; you actually don't have an opinion. . . yet. You are enjoying the freedom of not having to figure out how to help her or fix her feelings. You are controlling yourself. Keep it up; you'll be very glad you did."

Sarah continued, "I'm already tired enough of having my energy sapped by Rachel's problems and I don't want to go to a support group or to therapy because of my relationship with her." I privately congratulated myself again because that is what I would have suggested if I had not kept my mouth shut. It seems my daughter is making progress "letting go" of her sister. And I can see that I am making progress too in "letting go" of trying to fix my daughter and her problems with her sister. It not only feels supportive just to listen, but I don't suffer from pangs of guilt or the plague of second guessing myself after I hang up the phone. I guess at this stage in my life it is just too much trouble and takes too much time and energy to mentally regurgitate every comment in every conversation, in order to sort through the minutia of relationship issues.

∞

Becoming a Reflective Listener makes an impression on everyone, but especially on your children, no matter how old they are. This skill plays to their maturity. It reinforces that you have confidence that they can handle the responsibility and consequences of their decisions. Remind yourself that most unsolicited advice is perceived as criticism. The more you listen, give up outcomes, and echo their position, the more they will open up and confide in you. The more they hear themselves, the less they will have to defend their position. The less they have to defend themselves, the more their thinking can expand to see other options. Most support groups discourage "cross talk," which means commenting about what another speaker has said, or giving advice in the meeting. This is one of the basic reasons why 12-Step meetings work so well.

Jacob Weisberg, a behavioral consultant in California, conducts classes in Reflective Listening for families and business people. He narrates the story of a woman who was trying to tell her husband about something that was important to her. Hubby did not appear to be listening. As a matter of fact he had his head buried in the newspaper while she was talking to him. Finally, in a burst of frustration, she tore the paper from his hands and shouted, "You haven't heard a word I said!" He immediately turned to her with resolute eye contact and repeated, verbatim, everything she thought he had not heard. Weisberg asked his audience if they thought the woman felt better after she knew her husband had received her message. The answer, of course, is "no." The point is that *the feeling of being heard is more important than actually being heard!* He recommends that we adopt an empathetic listening model.

There are three easy steps to do this:

1) Lean forward toward the person talking.
2) Make direct eye contact.
3) Draw the speaker out by responding with "Tell me more,"
   or "I find that fascinating."

Communication experts will tell you that Active, or Reflective, Listening is the most critical component in establishing, maintaining and restoring relationships. Training involves listening for understanding. This is no easy task. Like professional psychologists or psychiatrists, we need to be strongly motivated to sacrifice our own agenda and set aside our boredom, our preconceived notions, and our judgments. We need a strong intention to enter into the other person's thoughts, feelings and perspective, to understand their hopes, desires and fears. This potent skill of "listening as an interested but impartial observer" is the sharpest arrow in your quiver when your target goal is to "win friends and influence people."

Voted most talkative girl in my high school senior class, practicing Active Listening has been a major challenge for me. Of course, it is much easier to be a better listener when I am not emotionally involved, but I also have more to gain, as well as more to lose, in these situations. And I find that "pride goeth before a fall" when it comes to this discipline. I am especially likely to fall back into my old pattern of expressing my unsolicited opinions when I feel urgency, anxiety or fear that "they" don't have the information they need to make the "right decision." And if I don't tell them, they won't get it!! My limited advances in this skill have come only through prayer, because my human nature is tempting me to do just the opposite.

∞

At this point I would like to momentarily digress from the topic of listening (I will come back to it shortly) and introduce you to some interesting new scientific information which is related to the topic of Active Listening. If you are in a personal or professional relationship with a person who has a mental illness and /or addiction you will be interested in reading I Am Not Sick, I don't Need Help, by Xavier Amador, Ph.D. Dr. Amador's research has broad implications for those of us who have been frustrated in our attempts to communicate with our clients, relatives and friends who have deny their illness or have the awareness of it, but are chronically treatment resistant. In the 1990's, Amador and his team identified three reasons for this most major obstacle which he calls "poor insight."

- The first is denial, which is a logical defense mechanism for a person who, understandably, does not want to give up the potential and promise of the life he or she had envisioned for himself or herself. From the patient's point of view he is simply being responsible for himself.

- The second is cultural influences wherein, for example, an individual may believe the condition is caused by "evil spirits" rather than brain chemistry.

- The third explanation for poor insight and lack of realistic self-concept is "Anosognosia," a medical term used to describe neurological deficits, particularly in the frontal lobe, which result in a "broken brain."

Regarding this "broken brain" concept, author E. Fuller Torrey, in Schizophrenic and Manic Depression Disorder, comments that "lack of insight about one's own bipolar or schizophrenia is not surprising, since the brain is the same organ that is affected in those disorders and the one we use to think about ourselves and assess our needs." This pathology was first observed in stroke patients who, accepted the facts of their condition but were unaware of their paralysis after their stroke. Due to cognitive deficits, they were unable to distinguish past abilities from current disabilities; many held on to the belief that they could function as well as before, despite all evidence to the contrary.

Since we all know someone, who may accept the fact of their mental illness but still be blind to the limitations of their condition, and is treatment resistant, this research is compelling. It is enlightening to entertain the possibility that sometimes "denial" and poor insight is physical instead of psychological. Thus the "broken brain theory" helps us get out of our "fault vaults" and begin a more objective approach to the communication process.

> *"...it is far easier to teach people ways to compensate for some forms of brain dysfunction than to change their personality."*

Here's the good news!! Dr. Amador reassures us that it is far easier to teach people ways to compensate for some forms of brain dysfunction than to change their personality. Amador recommends a collaboration model called "LEAP" (Listening, Empathizing, Agreement, Partnership) as a way of improving relationships and communication with a person who has "anosognosia," or broken brain syndrome, due to mental illness. Using this strategy the doctor and the family can become allies instead of adversaries.

- Listening involves walking in the other person's shoes to gain a clear idea of their experience of the illness and treatment.

- Empathizing involves understanding that if you want someone to seriously consider your point of view, you must be certain the other person feels you have seriously considered his. Quid pro quo. Keep in mind that empathizing is not necessarily agreement.

- Agreement involves focusing on making observations together and identifying facts you can agree upon.

- Partnership's objective is to collaborate on accomplishing the goals you have agreed upon and to become teammates against a common opponent.

Dr. Amador outlines the following guidelines as you begin Listening for agreement.

- Set aside time to talk.
- Agree on an agenda, even if it is to have no agenda.

- Listen for beliefs about the self and beliefs about the illness. Listen for fears, frustrations and desires. Listen for what motivates this person.
- Do not react.
- Let chaos be OK.
- Echo what you hear; no correcting, no matter how delusional or bizarre. Repeat exactly what is said. Don't omit what you wouldn't agree with. When you infer, make omissions or reality test you make a person feel alienated and create distance. Preface what you say with, "Let me be sure I understand you correctly. . ."
- Write everything down.

Some other strategies Amador recommends for keeping the individual engaged in the Reflective Listening process are:

> *"You can never argue a psychotic person out of their beliefs."*

1. Avoid both agreement and disagreement. Just continue to say " I would like to know more about that." Or, "why do you feel that way?" Don't be afraid that you're "buying in" to things that are not true. Don't worry about making the person worse. You can never argue a psychotic person out of their beliefs.

2. Never give your opinion unless you've been asked repeatedly. If you are asked a question that would cause conflict say, "I promise I'm going to answer your question but I want to understand you first. Would that be OK?" Or, "I want to wait because I want to hear more. In my opinion, your opinion is more important than what I think." Responses like these will keep the interaction going.

3. When you finally do give an opinion. Preface it with "I could be wrong but . . ." Apologize if need be. Keep a tone of humility. Delaying your opinion conveys respect and forces the other person to ask for it. Be a half step behind them.

You might think this is an impossible order without going back to school for a Ph. D., but a friendly "coach," a support group and practice will help a great deal. You will learn by trial and error, and you will get better at it the more you practice. Keep in mind that the sole purpose of the

Reflective Listening process is to build trust, step upon step, by crossing over into their side of reality. By empathetic engagement, you are quite likely to mirror to your client, relative or friend the dignity, respect and autonomy they crave. And, be assured, this method has been successful in drawing persons who have been resistant to medication into a cooperative treatment plan.

∞

Mona L.: I knew at a certain point I was slowly losing my grandmother to Alzheimer's because her conversation was becoming limited to about five topics from her past. Every time I saw her, it was as if there was a script for each history subject. It was a repetitive litany as if she was talking to a stranger who was hearing it all for the first time. She was most animated when she was telling me about the Bible stories her own mother had read to her when she was young, the happy times growing up in a small Michigan town, the memories of an unrequited love and her passionate insistence that if children aren't picked up when they are babies, they are damaged for life. I am bored, as if on a treadmill, but I listen, listen, listen. I am content that she still knows who I am and it makes her so happy that I am there.

THE MIRROR CHANNEL

...seeing with new eyes...

Finding faults in others blinds us to our own.

Luke 6:41-42

My pet peeves in life are traffic jams, waiting in line and impatient people!

Overheard on the Mirror Channel

Watch the kind of people God brings around you and you will be humiliated to find that this is His way of revealing to you the kind of person you have been to Him.

Oswald Chambers, from <u>My Utmost for His Highest</u>

Why do you look at the speck of sawdust in your brother's eye and pay no attention to the plank in your own eye? How can you say to your brother, 'Let me take the speck out of your eye,' when all the time there is a plank in your own eye?

Matthew 7:3-4

Mirror, Mirror, on the wall . . .
I'm my mother, after all!

Who knows???

Now we see but a poor reflection as in a mirror; then we shall see face to face. Now I know in part; then I shall know fully even as I am known.

I Corinthians 13:12

THE MIRROR CHANNEL

The Mirror Channel is a conceptual place to turn, especially when we become aware that the conflicts in our relationships seem to be repetitive. It is a way of thinking about our positive or negative emotional responses to another person's character or behavior. The Mirror Channel is designed for people who want to get honest and be more at peace with themselves and others. I have found that The Mirror Channel is where I need to turn when I have a resentment towards someone. It is also useful to go there when I see things around me that are disturbing, situations I don't like, can't change and can't control. Mirror Channel viewing is for people who are tired of trying to figure out who, or what, is right and would prefer to concentrate on feeling better.

In order to get to the Mirror Channel, we must bypass the other ways of viewing life's problems—for example, programs we find on the "Hopeless Channel," the "Why Channel" and the "How Channel." On these other channels we look at life as if it is something that happens to us. On the Hopeless Channel we spend most of our time complaining about what happens. The dialogue here, "I can't be happy unless he changes," is popular with those of us who perceives ourselves as victims. Intellectuals enjoy the Why Channel: "Why is this happening? Why did this happen to me?" They stay tuned for the evening news and the latest "reasonable explanations." We hope that finding the answer to the "why" question will make us feel better. If it doesn't, we switch to the How Channel. Here we spend enormous amounts of time and energy trying to figure out how to change a person, place or situation or how to control what might happen in the future.

"The problem with your picture is not the fault of your receiver."

We generally don't switch to the Mirror Channel until we have spent enough time on these other channels to see that, while their perspectives may have been informative, entertaining or useful in the past, now we are looking for healing.

When we observe our life situations on the Mirror Channel, we begin to see that the pictures on the screen, the experiences, and especially the relationship problems and patterns we observe, may be outward projections of our own inner state. They aren't random events transmitted from a hostile satellite somewhere up in the sky. In fact, if we've been paying close attention, we often see the message in print flashing across the bottom of the screen. "The problem with your picture is not the fault of your receiver." Few of us came into life with an instruction booklet for the Mirror Channel, so we sat in front of the fuzzy picture trying to manipulate everything outside of ourselves to clear it up. Sooner or later it dawns on us that we need to focus our attention on the transmitter—-ourselves.

Does this mean we are responsible for everything that happens to us? Absolutely not. This metaphor is just another way to "change the things we can" by a willingness to look at our relationship issues from a somewhat different point of view. The Mirror Channel isn't about right and wrong but about honest, impartial observation. This perspective regards "responsibility" as the "ability to respond," not blame. This is a looking glass to see our mistakes, learn from them, allow others to make mistakes and to learn from the mistakes that others make.

On the Mirror Channel we accept that God is sovereign. His creation has perfect order and purpose. There are no random accidents. We accept the fact that even though "bad things happen to good people," God loves each of us and desires that we grow closer to Him.

If you or I try to run away from a person or situation that was created to teach us spiritual lessons, we are quite likely to find ourselves in a similar conflict again. On the Mirror Channel we accept the idea that God allows imperfect people and imperfect situations to come into our life so that we will have more opportunities to grow into His image.

And we know that in all things God works for the good of those who love him, who have been called according to his purposes.
                                                                    Romans 8:28

After several years of watching The Mirror Channel, I have concluded that the projected images I see are my own fears, insecurities, and resentments, critical self judgments and blind spots. I have discovered that it is almost impossible for me to be disturbed by another person's behavior or attitude unless my judgment about them is reflecting self judgment in myself. I recognize three variations on patterns of judgment. If I am annoyed, irritated, angry, afraid or nervous around another person it is usually because:

1. I recognize in them a quality that I judge to be very negative; I am acutely aware of that same characteristic in myself, it makes me uncomfortable and I wish it would go away.

For example, I know that I am annoyed with penny-pinchers because I am often confused about whether I should be more generous with my money. I wish I could make my perceived short coming (whether it is true or immaterial) go away and I am most uncomfortable coming face to face with this quality in someone else because I don't want to be confronted with my "sin." I am judging them harshly because I am judging myself so harshly. Once I see the situation or person as a mirror image of myself, drop the self judgment, much of the emotional weight is lifted. I remind myself that Step Seven of any Twelve Step Program encourages me to turn my short comings over to the Higher Power. And the Bible reminds me not to judge others, for that is God's job too.

2. I criticize a behavior in other people that I secretly wish I could act out myself but I can't because I think it is not "righteous."

Does this person have something I want but afraid to go after it? I have observed that helpers, enablers and fixers may develop resentments against other relatives or co-workers when they get tired of doing the work all by themselves and run out of steam. They may be much more critical of other people whose primary purpose in life isn't to attend to the needs of others. They don't understand people who are not hard-wired helpers. Resentment and criticism are common reactions for martyrs who have decided they don't want to go to the cross alone. So instead of admitting they don't want to be a sacrificial lamb, they accuse others of being "unholy, unrighteous, selfish and self-centered." A more appropriate attitude would be to set aside blame and not be ashamed to ask for help.

I remember being angry and frustrated by my children's "irresponsible behavior" just at the time in my life when I was working so hard. From the perspective of the Mirror Channel I could conclude that they were reflecting my desire to be free from the burden of my adult responsibilities. My focus on "they aren't doing what they are supposed to be doing," helped me see that I was doing a lot of things I didn't have to be doing. I resented them because they were having fun. I had to acknowledge that I also had a problem. I needed to lighten up and let go of the idea that I have to take care of everyone else before I can have some fun. Was it an accident that when I became more permissive with myself, my irresponsible adolescent daughter became more mature?

3. I am very uncomfortable around people who exhibit a certain negative quality because I am unaware, and in denial, that I have that characteristic too.

Anthony deMello, SJ says:

Think of somebody you are living with or working with whom you do not like, who causes negative feelings to arise in you. Let's help you to understand what's going on. The first thing you need to understand is that the negative feeling is inside you. You are responsible for the negative feeling, not the other person. Someone else in your place would be perfectly calm and at ease in the presence of this person; they wouldn't be affected. You are. Now, understand another thing—-that you're making a demand. You have an expectation of this person. Can you get in touch with that? Then say to this person, "I have no right to make any demands on you." In saying that, you will drop your expectation. "I have no right to make any demands on you. Oh, I'll protect myself from the consequences of your actions or your moods or whatever, but you can go right ahead and be what you choose to be. I have no right to make any demands on you.

See what happens to you when you do this. If there's a resistance to saying it, my, how much you're going to discover about your "me." Let the dictator in you come out, let the tyrant come out. You thought you were such a little lamb, didn't you? But I'm a tyrant and you're a tyrant. I'm a dictator, you're a dictator. I want to run your life for you; I want to tell you exactly how you're expected to be and how you're expected to behave, and you'd better behave as I have decided or I shall punish myself by having negative feelings.

An example of this projection was a conflicted relationship with a boss that I had for ten years. I complained bitterly to others behind his back that he was overly critical, demanding and short on support. I was very sensitive to his "drinking problem." Only after I finally quit the job, (without really discussing any of my resentments with him directly), did I admit that I, too, had a drinking problem. Further, when I started running my own business and my own life, no one could have had a more relentless, self-critical taskmaster for a supervisor. His "short suits" were a mirror to my own.

All my life I have been very, very frightened of people who appear to be angry. Expressions of anger in my childhood home were not allowed; they were too dangerous. If my sister or I got angry with our parents or each other, we were told to go to our room until we could control ourselves. Of course, everyone was afraid that if the lid flew off, someone would get hurt. There was so much pent up rage in my muted alcoholic home of origin, it was not at all surprising I married a person who was also angry. Nor should it have been surprising that our son was born kicking, screaming and mad as hell.

Now the Lord is slow to anger, abounding in love and forgiving sin and rebellion.   Yet he does not leave the guilty unpunished; he punishes the children for the sin of the fathers to the third and fourth generation.

Numbers 14:18

Consider the effect of foul human waste that collects in the family's backyard septic tank. The problem is not that it is there; the problem is the cover-up. If no one ever acknowledges the darker side of human nature (some call it sin), no vehicle is sought to clean it up, remove or expiate it. Thus the garbage piles up. The stench can no longer be ignored and the younger generation has to deal with the whole overflowing mess. Perhaps so many of our children are anxious because they have inherited the legacy of alcoholism, sexual abuse, incest, addictions and mental illness which their parents denied. Ask any psychiatrist or psychologist what percentage of the people they treat for mental illness or addictions were sexually abused as children. Ask any person with a history of mental illness and/or addiction if they were sexually abused as children.

As deMello says we do not love or hate something about another person unless they reflect to us something we love or hate in ourselves. You might wonder how to look at the issue of abuse on the Mirror Channel. People who were abused often become abusers to compensate for their feelings of powerlessness, or are attracted to situations where they will abuse themselves by staying in those relationships. I've experienced abuse in many forms, as a child and as an adult. These interactions taught me to seek safety, love and approval from God, not from other people.

It took me many love affairs and many years of "husband hunting" to figure out it was no accident that I always ended up with "commitment phobic" gentlemen. Once I concluded that their reluctance was just a reflection of my own fears, and no one's fault, I ended up getting what I really wanted—I wanted to stay single.

Do not judge, or you too will be judged. For in the same way you judge others, you will be judged, and with the measure you use, it will be measured to you.

Matthew 7:1-2

A longtime friend who is a deacon in a large Episcopalian parish in Austin says they refer to troubled and troubling folks in their congregation as EGR's—Extra Grace Required. Perhaps the people that grate on our nerves are like the grains of sand that embed themselves inside our oyster. Doesn't it seem logical that God's plan is to create pearls that are priceless out of just such irritations?

RECEIVING
...being needy is not a shame...

Ask for what you want and don't be disappointed if you don't get it.
                                                            Jackie Castine

Ask, Ask, Ask. Ask later, ask someone else. Ask another way. Ask politely, ask with passion. Ask with a grateful heart and you will be heard.
                        Sarah Ban Braithnach, author of <u>Simple Abundance</u>

Ask for help and remember, asking for more information is not the same thing as asking for help.
                                        Tim Cusack, Motivational Speaker

We have to realize that we cannot earn or win anything from God; we must either receive it as a gift or do without it. The greatest blessing spiritually is the knowledge that we are destitute; until we get there our Lord is powerless.
                        Oswald Chambers, from <u>My Utmost for His Highest</u>

Ask, and it shall be given to you; seek, and ye shall find; knock, and it shall be opened unto you.
                                                            Matthew 7:7

RECEIVING

Do you know the difference between the Dead Sea and the Red Sea? The Dead Sea has no fresh water inlet. It is a closed entity and therefore not useful because it is stagnant. By contrast the Red Sea is spring fed. Because it is open to continuous free-flowing currents, it becomes a life-giving resource to living creatures. The moral of the story is that giving will soon dry up if there is no receiving.

Take a poll of the "givers and caregivers" in this world and see how amenable they are to asking for, and receiving, help for themselves. Usually, not very. They will say it is difficult for them to receive gifts. They don't want to put anybody out; they don't want to be the center of attention. They're often likely to be uncomfortable as a party guest if you don't give them a job to do. The Bible tells us "It is better to give than to receive." It expresses the spiritual truth that giving from the heart results in a greater gift to the giver than to the receiver. The corollary to that idea is that it is charitable to allow others to experience the joy of giving to you. It is charitable to receive charity.

Welfare has become a dirty word. Most people are ashamed of appearing needy. Often people are unwilling to accept a gift because they believe they are unworthy or that it has strings attached to it. We know that there is "no free lunch."

∞

May 20, 1990 was a bright sunny morning in Encinitas, California. I was having breakfast on my patio with a handsome man, a new friend, who was an evangelical Christian. I was about to receive the greatest gift I have ever been given. Actually, it had been offered to me at least five other times in my life but I wasn't ready to receive it.

I was raised in a family that, relatively unfaithfully, attended Methodist or Episcopalian churches. I was confirmed, had a Bible, knew the Apostles' Creed and considered myself a Protestant. Our family's real faith, however, was not in a "Higher Power," but in "Higher Education." We worshipped knowledge, subscribed to the doctrine of self-help and self-sufficiency. We "tithed" to the Ministry of Information.

I always said the only thing I didn't want to be, more than an alcoholic, was a "born-again Christian." It was not at all easy for me to accept that we are all born sinners, and even harder still to believe that only believers can go to heaven. As I like to say "there is no room in the 'Inn-tellect' for Jesus Christ." The Bible says we must be as little children in order to enter the kingdom. Only those who come to the conclusion that they are spiritually hopeless and helpless are ready to receive the Good News. No one would have guessed how desperately broken and needy I was on that Sunday in May. I was exhausted from running.

My surrender to Christ as Lord of my life was as much a surprise to me as when I had suddenly turned my first born child over to the care of God, in an act of utter defeat and desperation, some fifteen years before. In retrospect, I think I was just an over-inflated metaphysical fish that God had had on His line for a long time. Like the wise fisherman He is, He gave me years of free reign. When I was totally spent, He started putting enough pressure on the line so He could reel me in. By the time I was fifty years old, I could no longer resist the mighty net that catapulted me straight into the boat. My searching and fearless moral inventory from the Twelve Step Program helped me realize I could not forgive myself. I knew I had no answers. I recognized my need for redemption. I needed a Savior.

Like most fish that get hooked, I can remember the painful jolt of what I thought would be a pleasant experience. During a phone conversation with my ex sister-in-law in 1989, she quipped, "Jim told me he divorced you because you were selfish." Since I had been working on my "searching and fearless moral inventory during this period, the information was not a real surprise but hearing someone, who hardly knew me, say it out loud was a shock! "Selfish," the worst possible shortcoming for a person who considered herself a "giver!!" It was then that I knew there was no hope. I also knew I was no better or worse than anyone else. We are all selfish and self-serving. And more by nature than by choice. We are born self-absorbed because it is the prime survival instinct of human nature. If this isn't original sin, what is? How could I fix that? I couldn't. But the Good News was that God had already provided a way to fix the self-ness of my human nature which separated me from Him. All I had to do was believe that the Gospel message was indeed the Truth.

For God so loved the world that he gave his one and only Son, that whosoever believes in him shall not perish but have eternal life.

For God did not send his Son into the world to condemn the world, but to save the world through him.

John 3:16-17

And the side benefit was a relief as well.

Come to me all you who are weary and burdened, and I will give you rest. Take my yoke upon you and learn from me, for I am gentle and humble in heart, and you will find rest for your souls. For my yoke is easy and my burden is light.

Matthew 11: 28-30

Once I was "saved" there was a new peace and a new freedom. Just this year, I looked at a psychiatric evaluation of my adult son who recalls that, "When I was a kid, my mom dragged me around to all her friends. She complained and explained about my behavior problems but never said anything about her own." Was I surprised? Shocked? Disturbed? Not at all. I had done the housecleaning, been forgiven by God, forgiven myself and I had been declared "not guilty" because Jesus paid the price for me with His death on the cross. This is recovery and reconciliation for the Christian believer. I know also that all my children have forgiven me for being human and making mistakes, just as they live with the knowledge that God loves them in spite of their own shortcomings.

∞

The world may define independence as "healthy" but the Apostle Paul says otherwise in his letter to the Corinthians:

Now the body is not made up of one part but of many. If the foot should say, "because I am not a hand, I do not belong to the body," it would not for that reason cease to be part of the body. And if the ear should say, "because I am not an eye, I do not belong to the body, it would not for that reason cease to be part of the body." . . . But in fact God has arranged the parts in the body, every one of them, just as he wanted them to be. If they were all one part, where would the body be? As it is, there many parts but one body. The eye cannot say to the hand, "I don't need you!" And the head cannot say to the feet, "I don't need you!" . . . so that there should be no division in the body, but that its parts should have equal concern for

each other. If one part suffers, every part suffers with it; if one part
is honored, every part rejoices with it.
I Corinthians 12:14-16, 18-20, 25-26

God's plan is for us to become totally dependent on Him. Doesn't it make sense that if we had a closer relationship with God, we would likely find that our human relationships would be more Godly? And in our human interactions, God wants us interdependent, to experience both the giving and receiving, mutual give and take.

But as we resist dependence on God because of our human nature, we resist interdependence because of false pride and self-will. We want to go our own way. A friend of mine who is active in ministry was telling me about a retired Foreign Service doctor in their congregation whose wife was in the second stage of Alzheimer's. He refused help from parishioners, insisting that he could handle the situation himself. "I'm fine, we're fine," he always replied. He went out for a quick errand, was in a car accident and was taken unconscious to the hospital. She went out looking for him and was missing for two days.

∞

Linda B.: Remind your caregivers that what all human beings need in order to grow is the give-and-take of love. I was a "caretakee." I used to wish that my mother would get sick or show emotional weakness, leave some opening for me to do something for her. That opportunity did not come until her final illness. Although I did little physical caretaking of her (she was hospitalized or had home health care), my willingness to visit often kept her spirits up. "You've been very sweet to me," she said in her final blessing, "and I appreciate it."

∞

Author of <u>Please Don't Say You Need Me</u>, Jan Silvious notes that many Christians need to receive more of the spiritual blessings promised to them. She says, "Some zealous Christians want to do all they can to serve Christ, and they exhaust themselves in the process. It was to these that Jesus extended His invitation to go to Him and learn from Him. Jesus spent most of His earthly ministry surrounded by needy multitudes. He faced relentless opposition. He often prayed through the night and rarely had any privacy, yet he sought and received rest and strength from His Father. It was not that

Jesus did not work hard but that He knew the path to spiritual rest. Are you weary? Go to Jesus and let Him give you His rest. His rest will restore your soul as nothing else can."

∞

The following commentary on Psalm 23 came, without a credit, off the Internet.

The Lord is my Shepherd
That's Relationship!

I shall not want
That's Supply

He maketh me to lie down
in green pastures.
That's Rest!

He leadeth me beside
the still waters.
That's Refreshment!

He restoreth my soul.
That's Healing!

He leadeth me in the
paths of righteousness.
That's Guidance!

For His name sake.
That's Purpose!

Yea, though I walk through the valley
of the shadow of death.
That's Testing!

I will fear no evil.
That's Protection!

For Thou art with me.

That's Faithfulness.

Thy rod and Thy staff
they comfort me.
That's Discipline!

Thou preparest a table
before me in the presence of my enemies.
That's Hope!

Thou anointest my head with oil.
That's Consecration!

My cup runneth over.
That's Abundance!

Surely goodness and mercy
shall follow me all the days of my life.
That's Blessing!

And I will dwell in the
house of the Lord.
That's Security!

Forever.
That's Eternity!

HEALING
...passion for life...

But, taking time to live your own life and celebrate and do the things that are healing, you can just possibly save yours.

Judy Collins, author of <u>Sanity and Grace</u>

Recovery is not a fragile little circle undisturbed by life. It is recovery that rocks and rolls with life's punches! – Think for yourself, don't lie to yourself, and take control back, step by step.

Marty Raaymakers, <u>"Recovery That Rocks"</u>

True contentment is a real, even an active virtue—not only affirmative but creative. It is the power of getting out of any situation all there is in it.

G.K. Chesterton

If you can use what you have learned from your experiences to help even one other person overcome adversity, then you have squeezed some good from otherwise awful circumstances.

Bryan Golden, author of <u>Dare to Live Without Limits</u>

"For I know the plans I have for you," declares the Lord, "plans to prosper you and not to harm you, plans to give you hope and a future."

Jeremiah 29:11

The Physician

When I heard about your death, I thought
did he hoard his pills? Thank you for dying
of a "massive heart attack," not an overdose.

Dead of a broken heart, a heart broken open
like a geode to reveal its worth. For humility,
life held you in the gutter, face down;
stripped away your medical degrees,
your two sons, your wife.
Nothing remained. No hope of a personal life.

What sustained was service to "the alcoholic
who still suffered." As you, years sober,
suffered brain pan on fire, eyes burning,
cigarettes inhaled with a reckless fury,
yet lending a quiet hand to newcomers.
I remember thinking this man is a saint.

"We are not saints," our Book says.
In your dark suit, white shirt,
dressed for the office, putting in long hours
I see, if not a saint, a great doctor
who found his calling.

The coals of your eyes sparked sobriety
in many an extinguished soul.
Now you live the First Promise-
We are going to know a new freedom
and a new happiness.

Save me a chair in your new waiting room:
I need to consult you.
Freed of the violent tightrope
of up moods and down,
You radiate peace, dear physician and friend.

Linda Brown

HEALING

Pamela W.:   In 1982, I was diagnosed as "manic depressive" and I was hospitalized. During the next eight years I was constantly medicated and told by psychiatrists that I would need to take medication for the rest of my life. They said I was in danger of becoming psychotic if I did not cooperate with the treatment plan. I had been brought up to trust doctors. However, I found that the medications crippled my ability to think deeply or creatively or to remember the many associations that gave me pleasure. I tried to convince my doctor that I was functioning poorly, feeling drugged, lethargic and unable to enjoy my imagination or my life. I was also unable to control my weight. When changing drugs did not help, I tried changing doctors. This went on for eight years.

I finally found a psychiatrist who only did "talk therapy" and did not prescribe drugs. I learned how good nutrition and exercise could help me with my moods. I stopped taking all medications and have never started up again. My help came from people: from friends, family, teachers, self-help support groups, self-help, literature, my new doctor and myself. What about help from G_d? To me G_d is found everywhere on that list.

My recovery experience can be summarized as discerning the difference between "right and wrong thinking." I became adept at identifying my own errors in judgment, in experimenting with suggestions from other people, but trusting my own awareness and testing too. I learned to be cautious when I observed myself talking too rapidly; I learned to have extravagant buying binges with coins and dollar bills instead of big bucks. I learned to expect mood swings and to accept them gracefully without catapulting with panic into either extreme. I learned to focus on small improvements, not longed for transformations.

> *"I prefer viewing my life as an adventure story, instead of judging whether or not it is a "success."*

I did my best to avoid grandiose thinking, feeling special, loving "glitz," being impatient, repeating non-functional behavior and self-defeating habits. I find it helpful to my mental health to tolerate mistakes, imperfection, disapproval, anger, personal losses and periods of low energy and despair.

Having been a literature major in college, I had a lot of experience thinking in terms of character development, plot, themes and the possibilities for structure, beauty and congruence in fiction and poetry. Now I view my "life story" as a work in progress, as art to be shaped and explored. I am aware of its brevity, its mystery and all the choices I have to interpret what is going on. This way of thinking helps me stay in charge of my life and make my own decisions. I prefer viewing my life as an adventure story, instead of judging whether or not it is a "success."

∞

Darlene N.: My story is about sexual abuse which is happening every day, in every city all over the world and has been for centuries. It is a sickness that has no boundaries and leaves its victims dealing with the after-effects for most of their lives. For many of its victims, the molestation remains hidden for years.

I was first sexually abused by my step-grandfather when I was just four years old. It started with inappropriate touching but in time it ended up in rape. As a child I wished he would die so the pain would finally stop. He actually did die when I was eight and I was sure my wishful thinking was what killed him. With that in my head, just after his death I shut down inside and blocked off every memory of the abuse. But the abuse in my life did not stop there. When I was fourteen I met a boy through school. He started the sexual abuse all over again and it ended in rape also.

Several years later after my marriage, I talked to some friends about my past and they encouraged me to go into therapy. Soon I started having memories of the abuse from both men. I was unable to devote myself to the relationship with my husband and he soon filed for divorce. That same year my mother died, and I lost my job. I was at the point of telling God that I just couldn't take one more thing. I poured out my heart to God in prayer and begged him to help me get past all of this before I lost what little sanity I had left. But the memories continued and I had to relive the incidents from the perspective of a four-year-old.

It has taken strong determination to stay with the therapy and continue to heal. I had to go back and recoup the years of arrested emotional development. I have come to deeply appreciate the supportive and caring people who stood by me through this trial. The most profound change in my life has been how my relationship with God has grown and deepened as I have struggled to come to peace over the anger that God would "let this happen to me." The process was facing the hurt that had lived deep within, releasing the fear that I had done something wrong and to find answers to questions I was afraid to ask. I was forced to be completely honest with God, open my heart and trust that I could follow wherever He might lead.

∞

Loretta and Gary M.: A year ago our family was teetering on the brink of chaos. We have two boys, ages 16 and 13, both with severe emotional disturbances. The oldest had been diagnosed with early onset bipolar disorder, Attention Deficit Hyperactivity Disorder (ADHD), and chronic depression. He is gifted intellectually. His younger brother was also getting psychiatric help and was symptomatic of bipolar but not labeled as such. He cut himself on three occasions when highly stressed but was never hospitalized. He, too, has learning disabilities caused by a chemical imbalance. My husband and I had no relief from the constant care and monitoring which our children needed or from the enormous financial burden of psychotherapy for all of us. We were at the end of our rope when we heard about a community mental health provider in our county who offered home-based family therapy for children with serious emotional disorders.

At first we were skeptical and didn't think any program would work because our older boy was so thoroughly manipulative and intimidating. We didn't think anyone was tough enough to stand up to him. But it worked. Our highly skilled case manager helped our younger boy feel included yet protected and we finally received parental training in short term crisis intervention. Working with the in-home therapist gave me the confidence that I lacked as a parent; I no longer felt like I was being irrational and both my husband and I gained the confidence that gave us the control to follow through. As a consequence much of the overt manipulation is greatly reduced and conflicts are much less likely to escalate to physical proportions. Our eldest is now able to explain his point of view rationally as opposed to flipping out into aggression. Our younger son was recently selected as the most improved student of the month. Dinner time is a little calmer these days, too.

With our oldest's behavior as dramatic as it was, we lost a lot of friends along the way. I had come from an old fashioned faith. If you do what you're supposed to do, you'll be OK. When we had these "imperfect children," I thought God was mad at me. I thought I was supposed to be protected from all of that. But I have come to the conclusion that life happens, but it's faith that tells you how to handle it. Our twenty-year marriage has survived through prayer. It has been rough but we see that it will get better. We have a sense of humor too. We tell each other "You can't divorce me because I know you love me too much to leave me alone with the kids."

∞

Folksinger, Judy Collins acknowledges that her son's death by his own hand taught her many things and became her greatest teacher. "In the wake of his suicide I have had to face my own demons, take stock of myself, send out all the green shoots of life that might have withered and hold them in a fierce embrace against the stones and monuments of memory and the future. It has taught me to lock those shoots of green in the total grip of passion: MY PASSION FOR LIFE."

∞

Linda B.: About seven weeks before my mother's death, I came into my own adult power and was able to reassure her on her deathbed that I would not drink, smoke or overeat. I added weekly yoga classes to my acupuncture for emotional balance and arrived at the conviction I could take care of myself.

I sometimes wonder if my chronic depressions were a subconscious (but poor) strategy to shake her loose from trying to control my life. Perhaps if I depressed her enough, she would let go, stop giving advice or criticism, start using phrases like "It's your life" or "I'm sure you can figure out what to do," instead of "Mother knows best." We could have had more fun as friends, as equals, traveling together. As it was, we only took one trip together. I paid for it; I helped her with a book review for her book club; we shopped up one side of the street and down the other. Whenever I return to that mountain resort community, I have the happy memory of our rare camaraderie—the time my strong mother let me "do for her."

∞

Tom S.: Our Mom was in her mid-fifties when she had her first "breakdown." That's the term that was used up to that time for anyone who suffered from any psychiatric disorder. It's ironic that this is the same term we use to describe an automobile that quits running. Tow it in, diagnose the problem, and give the mechanic permission to "fix it!" Sometimes the repair takes and sometimes the fix is short-lived and the car goes back for a follow up session with the mechanic. It seems this is the way it works with diagnosing and treating mental disorders.

When I arrived at my parents' home that evening, it was apparent that my mom had been drinking, but her behavior did not seem to be totally alcohol induced. She was shouting obscenities and accusing my father of being Satan himself and made all kinds of outlandish claims of terrible things that had happened to her through the years. I had no idea what was happening, but I knew she needed help that I couldn't give her. I called my brothers and sisters and tried to fill them in on what was happening. Since two of my sisters were nurses, they had the greatest understanding of mom's condition, but there was some level of denial in all of us.

It was at this time I heard the term "manic-depressive" but had no real idea of the true nature of the disorder. She began her treatment and Lithium was prescribed to help control the disorder. With the exception of a few minor "incidents," the medication, along with her psychotherapy seemed to bring her back to a state of "normalcy" that we all could live with. The whole family became involved and made sacrifices to return home to help dad when possible.

Almost twenty years later, Mom stopped taking her lithium and began exhibiting even more bizarre behavior than before. She was still drinking well into her 70's, sleeping just a couple hours a night and running my dad ragged. This time we, the adult children, planned an intervention. We composed a letter to our parents about their unacceptable behavior, the effect it was having on them, and us, what we expected them to do and how we would support them. We figured, with all the facts laid out, my Mother would recognize her illness and my Father would become aware that he was enabling her through fear of her anger.

To our amazement and disappointment our plan backfired. Mom became more hostile and hateful, asking how we could say such terrible things about her. She said that she would rather have cancer than mental illness because it meant she was a bad person and that it was a punishment from God. She accused us of being ungrateful and evil children. Her eyes were cold, hollow, almost evil. I never before realized how a chemical imbalance in the brain could create such a personality change. Dad was almost impotent by fear and guilt because he knew she would take her wrath out on him when we left. He believed he had somehow caused her drinking and strange behavior.

"She said that she would rather have cancer than mental illness because it meant she was a bad person and that it was a punishment from God."

The three of us left after our brief visit feeling powerless. We updated our other five brothers and sisters and decided that the best thing we could all do was to visit whenever we could, continue to pray for them and put things in God's hands.

Following a brief involuntary hospitalization shortly after our visit, her mental health seemed to be the best it had been for years. But the next year her physical health began to deteriorate and she died in June of 2000. During the last days of her life, all of her children and grandchildren were able to spend time with her. We laughed and cried and shared stories of things she kept in her heart all those years. At the end, even in her pain, her eyes sparkled, replacing the hollow look of a few years earlier. There was no anger, no hate, only love. For those few special days, by the grace of God, and her unbelievable will to live, we had our Mom back.

∞

Elizabeth Y.: As Jackie's mother I have been invited to contribute to her book entitled "I Wish I Could Fix It, But . . ." I have spent forty-three of my ninety years living with active alcoholism. My own father was sober from the time I was two years old until I was fourteen. When he began to drink again he became a different person. He seemed angry, withdrawn and he often had temper tantrums. During the twenty years Jackie spent living in our family of origin, her father also was drinking regularly. I believe that the effect of this on me reflected on her.

Jackie is a fraternal twin. From the very beginning, the girls were very different in their personalities. I recall that even in the crib, Suzanne was placidly sucking her thumb and twirling her curly hair, while the wiry Jacqueline was climbing up and over the bars to get out. As they grew up, their differences became more evident. Suzanne was docile and quiet: Jacqueline was very active and talkative. In junior high school, Jackie's choice of friends was not as good as her sister's. She seemed more attracted to the less successful girls. At one time her father put a stop to one of the girlfriend relationships we disapproved of. This intervention led to a complete about-face in her behavior. In high school, she found new friends and made a concerted effort to be as successful as she could be with high academic achievement, honors and awards. This was the first time that bipolar behavior manifested itself, although it was not recognized as such at this time.

Her later dating years, marriage, child-rearing years, and divorce brought the usual ups and downs with the accompanying emotions which seemed to be extreme. During this time I was very absorbed in my own artistic work, so I wasn't paying very close attention. Each reversal in her life brought about a very strong effort to change. Her efforts to succeed, to be at the top, seemed excessive and led to exhaustion—again a pattern. The break-up of a long-term relationship came about during an intense involvement in a spiritual program. This resulted in a move across the country to California. New scene, new job, new close relationships,   etc., etc., etc...

She returned to Detroit when she was 54, again becoming very involved in another religious ministry.   This time she gave it all financially, everything she had, including all her retirement savings and the use of her credit cards.   It was this episode that brought her to the end of the line. Fortunately she was able to ask for help.   During her recovery she came to stay with me as a safe place. She applied herself to every avenue of help available—the pattern of diligence again.   My part in all this was primarily as an observer. My years in the Al-Anon program allowed me to be concerned, but detached.   I offered concrete assistance, such as room and board, and transportation when it was needed, but not advice. I was grateful that I could work my program and let her work hers. It is a great joy to observe the continuing progress of her recovery.

EPILOGUE

Six days before this book went to press, my troubled son, John, who, in spite of his probation, had been using marijuana and alcohol, stabbed himself four times in the chest and abdomen in his apartment. The neighbors called the police. They took him into emergency at a Los Angeles hospital.

Just three hours earlier I had spoken with him by phone. He told me he had given away his "stadium-sized" television to a Sobriety House. He said he wanted to get out of town, get a new start. He said, "Mom, they are out to get me, I have to get out of here, I won't let them take me down. I'm not going to make it." I asked him if he was depressed. He said, "Yes." I asked if he was thinking about suicide. He said, "Yes, again." He told me that I was the best mother in the world. I told him I loved him and that help was available to him. I gave him a hotline phone number to call.

I prayed that God's will would be done. I "let go." Then, I turned back to my "drug of choice," work. Three hours later, as I began to investigate the possibility of getting a court order, to have him committed in California while I was still in Michigan, I got the phone call that he was in the hospital. The police office who called me said he had lost a lot of blood but would recover.

He was under suicide watch and transferred two days later to a behavioral health psychiatric facility where he stayed only two more days before being released with prescriptions for antibiotics and vicodin. I tried, but failed, to speak to his physicians during the brief time he was there.

From our several phone conversations it seemed he had had a change of heart and mind. He seemed very repentant, very contrite and apologetic for how much heartache he had caused the family. When John told us he wanted to come east to be closer to family, all of us were afraid. His sister, who is also in recovery from both bipolar and addiction disorders, talked to him about her recent challenges. She made it clear that, while she understood what he was going through, he needed to get clean, sober and stable mentally where he was, especially since his probation would prevent a geographic move. He agreed.

I, too, had a change of heart and mind. When I described John's mental state as "delusional, paranoid, and psychotic," to my Goddaughter, she said,

"What if he is telling you the truth? What if he really is engaged in a battle with an enemy? As Christians, you know we believe that everyone of us is constantly waging a war against the devil who seeks to destroy us." She went on, "Satan is a reality, for us, not a metaphor, you know." Then she prayed, tearfully and passionately, as I could not. We acknowledged that there was indeed a spiritual battle going on for John's soul, (They don't call alcohol "spirits," for no reason!), and that, through intercessory prayer, we believed that the power of good will always overcome the power of evil.

The next time John talked to me about his enemies, I said, "I believe you." It was easy to "enter into his perspective," as Dr. Amador suggests, for I certainly could agree that "demon rum" and his drug addiction was life-threatening. Spiritually he was truly in the devil's playground and the battle was for his soul. Then he said, "I'm finally safe. I've been saved. Thank you, Mom."

As usual, my twin was my support lifeline to serenity. When I talked about my three hour delay attempting to intercede for him before he hurt himself, she said, "Don't even go there!"

But we, survivors of suicides and attempted suicides, always go there. The question is how long do we stay there? How do we get out?

Some may think it very strange that I could, or would, write about this situation when everyone's wounds are still so fresh. From a worldly perspective it may seem cold, harsh, uncaring, self-absorbed, and, especially, exploitive. I certainly had those thoughts myself. But as Charles Stanley says, "In a crisis we should be asking, 'What is God trying to do here?'"

As I considered my powerlessness over my son's illness, more than a continent away, and the Scriptures, I was reminded of how Jesus reacted to the urgent call for him to "come quickly" to heal his dying friend Lazarus in John 11. Jesus did not come quickly. He waited and then embarked on the two-day walk to Bethany and by the time he got there, Lazarus had been dead for four days. "Lord, if you had been here, my brother would not have died," said Mary, the sister of the dead man. The point of this story is that Jesus who was always in communion with His Father did not panic or experience a sense of urgency. The Son of God was "in the world, but not of it." He was not following the pleas of men but listening for God's guidance, God's timing and God's plan. God's plan was not healing but total resurrection of the body.

I had no plan for the ending of this book. The structure seems to have unfolded of its own accord. I see that the events of this past week have taken every member of my family, John, his sisters, my sister and me, through the valley of the shadow and into the spiritual promise of every topic in this book. We used our relationship with our Higher Power, prayers, and the 12-

Steps to take "one day at a time." Each of us, in our own way, experienced helplessness, acceptance, detachment, letting go in trust, fear, guilt, love, helping when we could and telling the truth when we couldn't. We gave and we received. Each of us had new insights and heard new wisdom—the true meaning of the word "repentance." We experienced pain and healing.

∞

Post Script
June 2006

And there were more miracles of reconciliation for our family this past year. Some people get their grandchildren by means of the stork, others by signed adoption papers and/or trips abroad. I got my 7th grandchild this year by way of the telephone. Her Mother located me via the Internet and thus I flew to Austin, Texas to meet the lovely 14 year old granddaughter, I knew existed, but had never met. A few weeks later my prodigal son, John, was reunited with his daughter whom he last saw when she was three.

I never cease to be amazed at God's timing. Within months after the diagnosis and co-occurring treatment of his drug addiction and bipolar disorder, John was presented with an opportunity to be a presence in his daughter's life. Although it consists primarily of telephone conversations at this time because they live in distant cities, my son, a gainfully employed welding inspector, is proud and happy to be able to pull out the check book and indulge her on a regular basis.

For now, it seems that the life long drama of our crisis ridden relationship has been reduced to mundane Sunday afternoon phone updates like the one left on my voice mail last week.

"Hi Mom, John here. Everything's OK with me. Nothing spectacular or exciting. Just another work week. I'm on a school job. It's expected to last for awhile. I'm looking forward to that. Let's see, what else? Getting high 80's, low 90's on all my tests for advanced certification. Keepin' out of trouble, stayin' clean, takin' my meds and cuttin' back on my smoking. And so everything's good."

EPITAPH

For now we see in a mirror dimly, but then face to face;
now I know in part, but then I shall know fully just as I am known.
But now abide faith, hope, love, these three:
but the greatest of these is love.

I Corinthians13:12-13

EPITAPH

Johnny Weld
September 20, 1961 – October 30, 2007

Reprint from the November 20, 2007 Detroit Free Press Editorial Opinion

Understand the Behavior and Mental Illness Link
By Jacqueline Castine

Mitch Albom's sensationally headlined Sunday feature story, "Is there a murder plot in your child's head?" poses the question, "How can anyone explain this story?"

As the community education specialist for the Oakland County Community Mental Health Authority and the mother of an adult son with a long psychiatric history, I welcome this "teachable moment" because there is so little public understanding of the correlation between behavioral disorders, mental illness, substance abuse and brain disease.

Albom reported the details of 16 year old Cory Ryder's attempts to hire a gunman to kill his parents. He described the teen's severely disturbed developmental history, the litany of his parents' attempts to fix him, and the varied environmental family and social ills that are all too commonly addressed. Albom expressed amazement that this Mother could still embrace her boy.

Maybe in spite of the fearful nights and guilt filled days, Cory's mother had become educated that severe behavioral abnormalities can be symptoms of organic brain dysfunction. Maybe she learned that her son was born with a "broken brain" and that in spite of the psychiatric help he had received (but was not reported in this story), she, like me, became the enemy targeted by her son's psychosis. Perhaps her head was engaged as much as her heart when she treated him as if he was suffering from multiple fractures, cancer or another life threatening no fault illness.

The brain is the organ that controls the body, mind and spirit. Psychiatry is the branch of medicine that studies brain disorders. Psychiatric units in hospitals are now called Behavioral Health Units. While there is truth to the fact that "misbehaviors" in both adults and children are not always biological or neurological in origin, it is critical that we attend to the distress signals of severe abnormal behavior as possible faulty brain functioning, often genetic. Family involvement, education, improved communication skills and counseling are adjuncts to recovery, not the cure for an organic illness.

Study and advanced treatment of broken brains is in its infancy. I have very recently lost my own son to suicide. At 46, he could no longer endure the torment of living with a mind out of control. His major symptom, starting at age 3, was rage, both outer directed and self destructive. In spite of his congenital disease and my maternal limitations, he had many successes, joys and achievements in his life. Brain disorders also have their mysterious remissions. He was educated, intelligent, handsome, funny and very passionate about sports. As a memorial to his life, I invite the public to learn more about mental illness, the third leading cause of death in young people and to support funding for the treatment and research of brain disorders.

Jacqueline Castine is the community education specialist at the Oakland County Community Mental Health Authority. She can be reached at jycastine@comcast.net

∞

<u>**Reprint from the May 2, 2008 Detroit Free Press Editorial Opinion**</u>

Was it Suicide? Shsssh. Don't Ask, Don't Tell.
By Jacqueline Castine

"He died after a long battle with a chronic illness," someone suggested as an obituary for my 46 year old son who committed suicide in a New Mexico desert last fall. It was his fifth attempt.

While it was essentially an accurate statement, I found it so understated as to be offensive. As his mother and a mental health educator I must expose, not cover up, the invisible "dis-ease" that took his life. It is imperative for me to transform my helplessness and grief over his chronic mental illness into a catalyst for change in the public perception of brain disorders and addiction. Perhaps this will forge a legacy to his life.

Too few people remember the front page photographs in 1966 when Emmet Till's mother staged an open casket in Chicago for public viewing, after her fifteen year old son was brutally murdered by racists in a dusty Mississippi town. She boldly used her son's bloody corpse as Exhibit A of racial injustice to end the apathy of this national disgrace.

I, too, am seeing red. Nobody wants to talk about suicide. The stigma, shame, and suffering are, for most, unspoken. My son was what is known as "a cutter." He repeatedly cut his wrists, deeper each time. Finally, he cut his throat.

Because I believe "the pen is mightier than the sword," my rage and heartbreak compel me to splatter some shocking, gruesome statistics about suicide across the pages of your newspaper.

Do you know that 37,000 Americans die by their own hand each year, one every 16 minutes?   That suicide is the 10th leading cause of death in this country, the 3rd ranking killer of young people? That people age 65 and older accounted for 16 percent of suicide deaths in 2004? That of the nearly 16,000 violent deaths occurring in 16 states, 56 percent were suicides? And still, only those who have lost a loved one are moved to mourn, often in secret shame.

Suicide is most often associated with mental illness, especially clinical depression, addictions and substance abuse. 1 in 4 families in the U.S. live with a person who has mental illness and/or an addiction. Because these diseases of the brain reveal themselves as conduct, behavioral and mood disorders, condemnation, incarceration or fearful silence often replace diagnosis and treatment. Individuals with undiagnosed mental illness are more likely to end up homeless, indigent, in jail, or in the morgue, rather than in the Behavioral Health Unit of a hospital. Suicide is the ultimate conduct disorder.

Most persons diagnosed with cancer, heart disease, or diabetes jump at professional efforts to extend their life. "I'm not sick and I don't need help," is a common proclamation of the "broken" brain. This death-defying delusion is a major barrier to diagnosis and successful treatment.

We rarely hide the fact that a family member suffers from kidney failure or respiratory disease. We don't consider these moral failings. We spend millions on research every year to cure them. Yet, we still treat biological diseases of the brain as if they were defects of willpower or character.

May is Mental Health Month. The good news is that national and state wide initiatives for suicide prevention are on the rise. Mental health education is increasing. Suicide rates are declining among some age groups. Personal experiences of hope and recovery from suicide attempt survivors abound. But no one can do it alone.

We must all become educated to end the sensationalism, fear, isolation and stigma of mental illness. For crisis intervention, evaluation and access to treatment, contact your local county **community mental health agency.** For family education and local resources contact **www.nami.org.** To find hope and local recovery support groups check out **www.dbsalliance.org.** To fund mental illness research, click on **www.miraresearch.org.**and **www.narsad.org.** For more information go to **www.jacquelinecastine.com.**

Jacqueline Castine is the community education specialist at the Oakland County Community Mental Health Authority in Auburn Hills, MI. She is the author of I Wish I Could Fix It, But . . . Phoenix Publishers © 2005. She can be reached at jycastine@comcast.net

∞

SUPPORT GROUPS AND RESOURCES

Families Anonymous is a fellowship of people whose lives have been affected by the use of mind-altering substances in a family member or friend. Freedom from guilt, worry and hopelessness comes from listening to those who have shared similar experiences and found some answers. By attending meetings, studying literature, talking to other members, and working the Steps of the program, the situation suddenly or gradually looks different. Reactions begin to change. Members learn to face reality with comfort, related behavioral problems of a relative or friend. Any concerned person is encouraged to attend even if there is only a suspicion of a problem. Here the emotionally involved family can find help, even if the offending member is not yet ready to seek help.

Families Anonymous
P.O. Box 3475
Culver City, CA 90231
800-736-9805

Al-Anon Family Group Membership is open to all who have a close relationship to, or love for an alcoholic. The group purpose is to (1) develop intelligent understanding of the alcoholism (2) to live according to the principles of Al-Anon in order to acquire serenity (3) to meet regularly for the exchange of ideas and inspiration and to gain strength through prayer and meditation (4) to practice humility and tolerance in our daily living and (5) to welcome and encourage the family of the alcoholic to participate in the program and live more abundantly.

Al-Anon World Service Office
1600 Corporate Landing Parkway
Virginia Beach, Virginia 23454-5617
888-425-2666
www.al-anon.alateen.org

Alcoholics Anonymous® is a fellowship of men and women who share their experience, strength and hope with each other that they may solve their common problem and help others to recover from alcoholism. The only requirement for membership is a desire to stop drinking. There are no dues or fees for AA membership; we are self-supporting through our own contributions. AA is not allied with any sect, denomination, politics, organization or institution; does not wish to engage in any controversy, neither endorses nor opposes any causes. Our primary purpose is to stay sober and help other alcoholics to achieve sobriety.

Alcoholics Anonymous World Service Organization
Grand Central Station
P.O. Box 459
New York, New York 10163

Adult Children of Alcoholics is a 12-Step fellowship for men and women who grew up in alcoholic or dysfunctional families. Members identify with fear of authority, approval seeking behavior, inability to feel and express feelings. The solution is to keep the focus on yourself, free yourself from the past, take responsibility for your own life and become your own loving parent. This is a spiritual program based on action – coming from love that allows its members to restructure their thinking and heal themselves.

Adult Children of Alcoholics
Central Service Board
Interim World Service Organization
P.O. Box 3216
2522 W. Sepulveda Blvd., #200
Torrance, California 90505
(213) 534-1815

The National Alliance for the Mentally Ill (NAMI) is dedicated to the eradication of mental illnesses and to improvement of the quality of life of all whose lives are affected by these diseases. NAMI is a nonprofit, grassroots, self-help, support and advocacy organization of consumers, families, and friends of people with severe mental illnesses.

National Alliance for the Mentally Ill (NAMI)
Colonial Place Three
2107 Wilson Blvd., Suite 300
Arlington, VA 22201-3042
Main: (703) 524-7600
Fax: (703) 524-9094
TDD: (703) 516-7227
Helpline (800) 950-NAMI (6264)

The National Mental Health Association is the country's oldest and largest nonprofit organization addressing all aspects of mental health and mental illness. With more than 340 affiliates nationwide, NMHA works to improve the mental health of all Americans, especially the 54 million people with mental disorders, through advocacy, education, research and service.

National Mental Health Association
2001 N. Beauregard Street, 12th Floor
Alexandria, VA 22311
Phone (703) 684-7722
Fax (703) 684-5968
Mental Health Resource Center (800) 969-NMHA
TTY Line (800) 433-5959

The Depression and Bipolar Support Alliance (DBSA) is the nation's leading patient-directed organization focusing on the most prevalent mental illnesses—-depression and bipolar disorder. The organization fosters an understanding about the impact and management of these life-threatening illnesses by providing up-to-date, scientifically-based tools and information written in language the general public can understand. DBSA supports research to promote more timely diagnosis, develop more effective and tolerable treatments and discover a cure. The organization works to ensure that people living with mood disorders are treated equitably.

Depression and Bipolar Support Alliance
730 N. Franklin, Ste. 501
Chicago, IL 60610
Phone: Toll Free (800) 826-3632
Fax (313) 642-7243

Incarcerated Loved Ones, Family and Friends Support Group
P.O. Box 285
St. Clair, MI 48079
Phone (810) 989-6476
roofron@gct21.net

Mental Illness Research Association (MIRA) MIRA's purpose is to find cures for mental illnesses and other brain disorders through funding brain research. MIRA also works to educate and erase the destructive myths surrounding the stigma of mental illness that block proper diagnosis and treatment for millions of Americans each year.

MIRA
(800) 896-MIRA (6472
(248) 338-1299 (Office)
(248) 338-1599 (FAX)
E-mail: info@miraresearch.org
Web site: www.miraresearch.org

National Mental Health Information Center: www.mentalhealth.org
National Mental Health Association: www.nmha.org
The Bazelon Center for Mental Health Law: www.bazelon.org
Federation of Families for Children's Mental Health: www.ffcmh.org
National Alliance for the Mentally Ill (NAMI): www.nami.org
Emotions Anonymous: www.emotionsanonymous.org
Mental Health Net: www. mentalhelp.net
Schizophrenics Anonymous: www.sanonymous.org
Internet Mental Health: www.mentalhealth.com
Mental Health Infosource: www.mhsource.com
The Schizophrenia Homepage: http://www.schizophrenia.com
NARSAD: http://www.mhsource.com
IAPSRS : www.iapsrs.org
U.S. Surgeon General on Mental Health:
www.surgeongeneral.gov/library/mentalhealth
U.S. Department of Health and Human Services:
Substance Abuse and Mental Health Services Administration
www.samhsa.gov

BIBLIOGRAPHY AND RECOMMENDED READING

Al-Anon. *Twelve Steps Twelve Traditions.* New York: Al-Anon Family Headquarters, 1981.

Alcoholics Anonymous. New York: Alcoholics Anonymous World Services, Inc., 1976.

Amador, Xavier. *I Am Not Sick I don't Need Help.* Peconic, NY: Vida Press, 2000.

Casey, Karen. *Each Day a New Beginning.* Hazelton, MN: The Hazelton Foundation, 1982, 1991.

Castine, Jacqueline. *Recovery from Rescuing.* Deerfield Beach, FL: Health Communications, Inc., 1989.

Chambers, Oswald. *My Utmost for His Highest.* Westwood, NJ: Barbour and Company, Inc., 1973.

Collins, Judy. *Sanity and Grace: A Journey of Suicide, Survival and Strength.* New York: Jeremy P.Tarcher, Penguin Group, 2002.

Families Anonymous, Inc.: *Today A Better Way.* P.O. Box 3475, Culver City, CA 90231-3475

Fink, Candida, M..D., Joe Kraynak. *Bipolar Disorder for Dummies.* Hoboken, NJ, John Wiley & Sons, Inc., 2005

Flach, Frederic F., M..D.. *The Secret Strength of Depression.* Philadelphia & New York, J.B Lippencott Co. 1974

Fawcett, Jan, M.D., Bernard Golden, Ph.D. & Nancy Rosenfold. *New Hope for People with Bipolar Disorder:* Roseville, CA. Prima Health, a Division of Prima Publishing, 2000.

Lerner, Harriet Goldhor. *The Dance of Anger: A Woman's Guide to Changing the Patterns of Intimate Relationships.* New York: Harper and Row Publishers, Inc. 1985.

Light for my Path: Illuminating Selections from the Bible. Ulrichsville, OH: Humble Creek, 1999.

Livingston, Patricia H. *This Blessed Mess.* Notre Dame, Indiana: Sorin Books, 2000.

Miklowitz, David J., Ph.D. *The Bipolar Survival Guide.* New York & London, Guilford Press, 2002

Oliwenstein, Lori. *Taming Bipolar Disorder*: New York. Psychology Today: The Penguin Group, 2004.

Peck, M. Scott. *The Road Less Traveled: A New Psychology of Love, Traditional Values and Spiritual Growth.* New York: Simon & Schuster, Inc., 1978.

Random House Dictionary of the English Language, Unabridged Version. New York: Random House, Inc., 1968.

Rodale, Jerome I. *The Synonym Finder.* New York: Warner Books Edition, Rodale Press, Inc., 1978.

Silvious, Jan. *Please Don't Say You Need Me: Biblical Answers for Codependency.* Grand Rapids, Michigan: Pyranee Books, Zondervan Publishing House, 1989.

Twelve Steps and Twelve Traditions: An Interpretive Commentary on the A.A. program. New York: Alcoholics Anonymous World Services, Inc., 1976.

Woman's Study Bible: The NKJV. Nashville: Thomas Nelson Publishers, 1979, 1980.